How His *Light Shines* Through Us

"This Is My Story"

"Standing Firm"

SHERRI LAND

Started These Writings on the day of: September 16, 2018
Completed These Writings on the day of: November 9, 2023

WestBow Press books may be ordered through booksellers or by contacting:

WestBow Press
A Division of Thomas Nelson & Zondervan
1663 Liberty Drive
Bloomington, IN 47403
www.westbowpress.com
844-714-3454

One scripture quotation from the:
Holy Bible NLT © 2020 Tyndale House Publishers
Cover Design and Photo by: Sherri Land Copyright © 2024
Poems by: Sherri Land Copyright © 2017, 2020, 2021, 2022
Photos taken by: Sherri Land Copyright © 2024
Photo of Snowflake taken by: My Daughter 2016. Used by permission.
Sketched images by: Sherri Land Copyright © 2024

All Scripture quotations unless otherwise indicated are taken from the: Spirit-Filled Life Bible Copyright © 1991 by Thomas Nelson, Inc.
The Holy Bible, New King James Version Copyright © 1982 by Thomas Nelson, Inc.
The New King James Bible, New Testament Copyright ©1979 by Thomas Nelson, Inc.
The New King James Bible, New Testament and Psalms Copyright © 1980 Thomas Nelson, Inc.

ISBN: 979-8-3850-2638-8 (sc)
ISBN: 979-8-3850-2640-1 (hc)
ISBN: 979-8-3850-2639-5 (e)

Library of Congress Control Number: 2024914148

Print information available on the last page.

WestBow Press rev. date: 9/26/2024

WESTBOW
PRESS®
A DIVISION OF THOMAS NELSON
& ZONDERVAN

How His
Light Shines
Through Us

"This Is My Story"

SHERRI LAND

"From His Glory,
For His Glory,
None Other"

In Dedication to God
To Lift God Up and Glorify Him

Without the Hope That the Lord Jesus Christ Brings To This World,
We Would Not Have Eternity In Heaven, To Look Forward To.
Oh What a Difference This Hope Brings!
Thank You Jesus, For All Your Help, In All Things I Do!
May He Be Glorified!
May All Who Read Be Blessed!

In Appreciation to the Following:

A Huge Thank You To: My Husband
For All His Help, Support, Encouragement & Patience;
In All These Adventures, That I Feel God Has Given Me To Accomplish.

A Special Thank You To: My Mother
For All Her Encouraging Words, Consistent Prayers for Me,
Leading Me to the Lord and Inspiring Me to Follow Jesus.

A Heartfelt Thank You To: My Dad
For Inspiring Me in Art and Music; For Guiding Me in a Career Field;
As Well As Being a Protective and Watchful Father over My Younger Years.

I Am So Thankful For All Of You!
Love You All So Much,
Sherri

A Sincere Thank You To:
All Who Have Shown Their Support to Me On This Journey!

For All These Things, I Am Truly Grateful!

To
My Children
And
My Grandchildren,

May you always keep God, first in your heart.
May His blessings be on you, each day that you start.
May you follow the path, He has predestined for you.
And may He bless you with,
Love... Peace... Courage... Strength... Compassion
And Wisdom as you follow, your journey through.

Love You All So Much!
Mom / Grandma Sherri

"May God Bless You All, As You Are Nourished, By His Word"

"But Jesus looked at them and said to them, 'With men this is impossible, but with God all things are possible.'"
Matthew 19:26

"You will keep him in perfect peace, Whose mind is stayed on You, Because he trusts in You."
Isaiah 26:3

In Memory of
Shirley Marie Kehler

Table of Contents

Poems

Life Is a Journey

Don't sweat the little things, Let us Pray over all things,
And never worry about anything,
This is my hope for us; that I pray, all the day through.
Life is a journey, we are merely passing through.
The goal is to enjoy and spread God's word too!

So let not our time, which is so precious,
Be wasted on worrying over life's daily messes.
Let us hold our heads high and enjoy the pleasure,
Of each breath we breathe and our days so unmeasured.
Always count our blessings each and every day,
And when negativity comes, just push it away!

So then, whenever a mountain does come our way,
Always remember, to reach for the Heavens and pray.
Life's not easy; God never promised it would be.
Therefore, let us leave our troubles at the feet of Jesus;
Then, Trust Him And Believe!

August 3, 2012
Updated for the purpose of this book on: November 1, 2023

"Be anxious for nothing, but in everything by prayer and supplication, with thanksgiving, let your requests be made known to God; and the peace of God, which surpasses all understanding, will guard your hearts and minds through Christ Jesus."
Philippians 4:6-7

Introduction

Dear Reader,

My hopes in writing this book are to tell my story of what I feel God is doing in my life. My goal is to hopefully inspire others to seek God, and to encourage others to search for their predestined God given gift and purpose in their own lives. I believe that what God is doing in my life is a wonderful thing; and I am so energized and blessed to be doing the work that I feel God has called me to do! When I changed my focus, and my search, to be totally seeking what God's will was for my life, everything seemed to shift and change to have more spiritual meaning. I believe that God has given me an outpouring of scripture based poems; and I feel that He has given me all these words in poem format to share with others. For me to close my handwritten journal, and put it away, just doesn't seem to me to be the right thing to do; when I believe that God has given me them to share with others. I am listing these poems in the order of the dates in which they were written; so that it may show how fast and frequently they came to me. I have written additional poems that are between these dates, which are not recorded in this book; I am only sharing the words to the poems that I have turned into songs to date. The song creation process did not fall in the same date order as to when the poems were originally written. Other poems that I have written, which are not included in this book, will possibly be a project for the future; if God is willing. I am currently working on my fifth CD alongside while writing this book; praying God will continue to help me through all of these projects.

I am also sharing some of my photos; I love taking pictures of nature. I hope that these pictures will be inspiring, and an encouragement for us to always be looking around; God is always showing off in His creation, it is quite wonderful to observe!

I have also included a few of my sketches. I love to sketch, it is very therapeutic! I highly encourage searching out what you love to do, and then find time to enjoy the gifts that God has gifted you with; then find ways to Glorify God with them.

"Nor do they light a lamp and put it under a basket, but on a lampstand,
and it gives light to all who are in the house."
Mathew 5:15

My prayer is that these writings will land in the hands of those which God has planned it to; That my story will encourage whoever is reading it to move forward with what they feel God is calling them to do; That it will accomplish all things that God has willed it to; And I pray for God's Blessings over this book. Thank you so much for your precious time which you have taken to read my book!

I Pray That God Will Bless You In All That You Are Destined To Do!
Sincerely,
Sherri Land

"Trust in the Lord with all your heart, And lean not on your own understanding;
In all your ways acknowledge Him, and He shall **direct** your paths."
Proverbs 3:5-6

God Doesn't Give Up On Us

I was born in the year of 1960, in the northern part of the state of Kansas. I have two brothers, one older and one younger. As far as I can remember back – I have always been a Christian. My mother has always made sure, through our younger years, that we were in church every Sunday; and my dad always taught us to be honest, and that telling a lie was worse than whatever it was, that we had done wrong. My mother has told me – that one day long ago – when I was about six years old, that I had asked her to pray with me; that I wanted to be saved. She said, that I had said to her: *"I wanted to ask Jesus to come and live in my heart."* I am so sorry to say, that I don't really remember this; but I do remember always trusting Jesus, whenever I needed His help, for as far back as I can remember. I remember praying for things as a child, and God always seemed to work things out to answer every prayer that I ever remember praying, except one; which I will write about a little later on in this story.

I have never written a book before; but I am going to attempt to do it now, for God's Glory, not mine. My hope is to help others, to be inspired to turn their full focus to God first, over everything else. I hope to also encourage others to see, that the only true way to fill that empty spot in our lives, is with Jesus. As well as to raise God high, so that we can see Him, and to know that we were created to be in close communion with Jesus Christ our Creator and Father in Heaven; and that *we need* the Holy Spirit living within us, to help guide us and direct us in the way that we should go. We will all, at some point in our lives – try to fill that void within us, with things that this world offers and promises to make us happy. But the truth is – it is impossible to have – genuine joy, absolute contentment, soul fulfilled love, and true peace, apart from Jesus.

I didn't realize this truth as much through previous years. Like I said – I have been a Christian for as long as I can remember; but, did I ask God for direction and guidance when making decisions through my life? No, I did not. Did I read the Bible every day? I did not. Was I even going to Church on a regular basis after leaving my parent's house, getting married, and starting my own life? I had not. Did I make sure that my own kids were in Church every Sunday, like my Mother had done for me? No, I hadn't. I have made some mistakes through my lifetime, as we all have, and I am sorry for that; but unfortunately, I can't change the past. All I can do now, with God's help, is to try to do better in the future.

But, if I had been putting God first – and if I had been asking Him for help and direction in my life – just maybe I might have figured out, what *my God given purpose was in life,* many years ago. Why did God create me? How much time have I wasted by not pursuing God, and not seeking what His will was for my life? What was I not getting accomplished for Him? In short, I was not living for God like I should have been; I was not putting Him first in my life, and I was not getting spiritually fed on a regular basis.

Did I love Jesus – absolutely, with all my heart! I was just not seeking Him as I should have been; I was not seeking what He had for me. But, you know what, even while I was not on the right path as I should have been, God never left me – God has always been faithful to me! Not because I deserved it, by no means; but because He is God and that is who He is, a Good God; and He loves me and He loves you! He is a faithful and loving Father to all of us! Although I wasn't chasing Him, I strongly believe that He was still chasing after me, and I thank Him so much for that! Thank goodness that He is so full of Grace, and loves us so much, that He never gives up on us; that He gives us time to get things right with Him. Thank goodness for this time of Grace that we are in, *these current days*, when we still have time to ask Him to forgive us of our sins. This time of Grace where we are still given the choice, and the freedom, to ask Him to be our Savior and Lord; and to invite Him to live within us, and to lead us into Eternity to live with Him forever and ever in Heaven. Thank goodness that His desire is that, not even one of His children, be lost and left behind.

He Has Rules for Us to Protect Us

I have learned through the years that God doesn't have rules for us because He is mean, and doesn't want us to have fun; He has rules for us to protect us. You see – God knows all things – and He wants to protect us from harm; His desire is for us to have life abundantly.

"For I know the thoughts that I think toward you, says the Lord, thoughts of peace and not of evil, to give you a future and a hope. Then you will call upon Me and go and pray to Me, and I will listen to you" Jeremiah 29:11-12

I met my husband in my senior year of high school, and we were married in the summer of 1978. God has blessed us with two awesome children, what a blessing they both are; God is so good! In 1983, my Husband joined the Air National Guard, and in 1984 we moved from our home town, to the big city of Wichita in the state of Kansas. Our two children were ages two and five at that time, and we were moving to a city where we knew no one! Our intent though, was to move to Wichita temporarily, just for a year or two, so that my Husband could accumulate work experience; then we would move back to our home town, to be close to family.

I prayed, and I prayed, and I prayed – for this dream to come true but God never answered this prayer. This is the prayer that I spoke of earlier, the one prayer that God never answered. After several years of trying to move back home – we finally gave up on that dream. Sometimes God doesn't answer all of our prayers – because maybe it just wasn't the best thing for us – I don't know. I have always lived my life with the saying that – *"All things happen for a reason"* – and this was one of those times that I had to *trust* the answer that I had received. I had to *trust* Jesus, and *trust* that He had something else planned for our lives, and that Wichita was where we were supposed to be.

God has answered many additional prayers for me, since way back then. He is so *faithful,* and I trust Him with my life, whether the answer is yes, or if the answer is no; because, I know that His answer, is the best one for my life.

I hate to bring any darkness into this story but unfortunately, it is part of our reality; you know, since Adam and Eve sinned in the Garden of Eden – which is recorded in Genesis (the first book of the Bible). Now, every day since that moment in time, we have had to deal with the results of their disobedience to God. I bring this up because, in the same way that the devil lied to Adam and Eve to get them to disobey God, is also the same way that the devil tries to deceive us today, as well. The devil's goal is: to divide, conquer, tear apart, and destroy us, in any way that he can. The devil will figure out our weakness, or whatever may be our biggest fear, and he will use it, to tear apart families, break our spirit, and destroy our confidence; any way that he can bring us down, he will. And, any way that the devil can keep us so busy, that there is no time to spend seeking God, and no time to spend learning about God – so that we may know who God is – he, the devil, will certainly do, just that! We have to always be on guard; we have to understand his tactics, and we need to know what God says about all of it. We can't give the devil a foothold – because that is all that he needs; he'll take it and he'll run with it! But – *When we reach up high for God's help* – God turns things around to the good, and with that being said: "*This is how his light shines through us – and this is my story.*" I have written a few poems here and there – but nothing anywhere close to what I am about to share now!

We All Will Come To a Crossroad

Every one of us, at some point in our lives, will come to a crossroad; where the devil figures out our weakness, when he learns how he can take us down, or upset us the most. It doesn't matter what it is, it could be something as little as a weakness of worrying too much, or it could be something really bad – which is horribly harmful for us. It makes no difference what it might be, because the devil will lie to us, and make it seem huge, whether it really is or not. He will make it seem so huge, that it will cause so much disruption in our life; in an attempt to destroy us, and every relationship that we hold dear, and anything that matters to us that is good. His constant pestering with his lies will be like a fly on your food, or a gnat in your face, that just won't go away; he can be very persistent and very annoying! Wherever we may see relationships falling apart, or disruptions in life – which are bringing no good thing about – we can be one hundred percent sure, that the devil is the source of the problem!

It is when something happens in our lives – that brings us to our knees that we reach up high! When we are at our weakest moment in life: That is when the devil will attempt to attack us, that is when he shoots his fiery arrows; and that is the moment in our life – when we are at a serious crossroad! We can either let the devil drag us into the deepest pit we have ever been in, in our life, and let him tear everything that is most important to us totally apart, and I promise he will do just that, with his lies and deception. He will cause us to think things are real that are not. He will twist incidents to mess with our mind. He is not for us, he is against us! He wants to destroy us, and every relationship that we hold dear. He will tear marriages apart, families apart, and friendships apart; he does nothing good! Nothing! The Bible says he is the father of lies: "When he speaks a lie, he speaks from his own resources, for his is a liar and the father of it." (John 8:44) The Bible also describes the devil as a thief:

> "The thief does not come except to steal, and to kill, and to destroy. I have come
> that they may have life, and that they may have it more abundantly."
> John 10:10

When we encounter the devil at this level, no matter what our weakness is, this is when we have to make a choice. We are either going to continue to listen to the devil and his lies, and let him destroy everything, or – we hit our knees and lift our hands up high, and pray for God's deliverance from the evil one! We will pray for God's divine protection! We will pray: *"God, please take this from me, I can't deal with this on my own!"* That is when God will do great things in our life; this is when He will work through us, in a way in which, we would have never imagined. This is the choice that I pray we all would take, to reach for God to intervene, and don't listen to the devil's lies. When we turn to God for help, when we reach up high, with all that we have in us, that is when our focus changes; and then we can start to hear what God has to say to us. It is at this pivot point, when the devil's lies become very clear as to what they are, just lies; and it is also when the devil loses his power over us! At this crossroad, he can no longer drag us into that pit!

God lifts us up and *out of the pit,* and He sets us up high, so that we can see things as He views them. Then things of the devil's power fade away. Good things enter, things that bring *Peace, Joy and Happiness,* the good things that God gives us. Relationships get repaired, and families are at peace, and joy is restored, as God intended life to be in the beginning!

"I waited patiently for the Lord; And He inclined to me, And heard my cry. He also brought me up out of a horrible pit, Out of the miry clay, And set my feet upon a rock, And established my steps. He has put a new song in my mouth-- Praise to our God; Many will see it and fear, And will trust in the Lord."
Psalm 40:1-3

Sometimes God allows some things to happen in our lives – but it is so good to know what scripture says about these things; then we can have *hope,* knowing that God will turn it around. Yes, He will turn it around to the good for sure, when we are trusting in Him! We can definitely trust our God during these times in our lives!

"But as for you, you meant evil against me; but God meant it for good, in order to bring it about as it is this day, to save many people alive."
Genesis 50:20

We all will have a day, somewhere along the way, when that devil will try to drag us into a pit, a crossroads, you may say. Where we will have to decide, am I going to let the devil continue to lie to me, or – am I going to search for the truth, the real truth, of why am I here? What does God have to say about it, and what is my purpose here on this earth? *"There surely must be something better, that I can be doing, rather than listening to such lies that the devil spews."*

As you may have figured out by now, this was my pivot point, my crossroad. This was the point where I realized, that I didn't have near enough of *God's Word, God's Promises,* and daily *Scripture* in my life, and in my routine. I was very vulnerable, very much caught off guard, and so not prepared. Although, I had been a Christian all of these years; I wasn't being fed Scripture daily, and I was not spiritually strong. I was a perfect target for the devil's deception – and he almost won!

Like I had said earlier on in this story, I have been a Christian for as long as I can remember. And having been raised, and brought up in a Christian church, I knew that there was Hope, and that I could reach for God's help – and I did just that, with all of my heart – and with everything that I had in me! And God is so *faithful*, as He has always been, through all of my years; He stepped into my life **big time!** He gave me a clear path ahead, and a straight road to follow. God's wonderful *Word* – will keep us on the right path! I am so thankful for *His Word!*

"Your Word is a lamp to my feet And a light to my path."
Psalm 119:105

"God's Path, God's Sky"

Jesus Please

Jesus, Jesus, Jesus
Please keep that old devil away.
Oh I pray, I pray, Oh I pray
Master, Savior, Jesus
Please keep me safe night and day.
When these old negative thoughts come my way,
Please fill my heart with all the promises You say.
Oh I pray, Oh I pray, Oh I pray
Please give me peace that forever will stay.
Oh I pray, Oh I pray, Oh how I pray.
My heart fills with sorrow,
How saddened I get.
Oh please, Oh please, Oh please take it away.
Please fill my heart with all the good things You give.
And please keep them there all the days that I live.
Oh I pray, O I pray, Oh… How I Pray!
Love You Jesus!

September 12, 2013

Thank God for Our Trials

When I started putting God first in my life, when I changed my focus to be totally on God, seeking Him, and what His will was for my life, and reading my Bible whenever I could – God started working through me – in an awesome way! With an outpouring of poems, I guess you could say. "And we know that all things work together for good to those who love God, to those who are the called according to His purpose." (Romans 8:28) You see, I believe that God allows some things to happen in our lives sometimes, to get our attention; and He definitely got mine! If things were perfect all the time, we would never realize that we needed Him. We would think that we were self sufficient, or that is what we would believe anyhow; and that is a very dangerous place to be! Because, when each of our days are through on this earth, we cannot save ourselves from the destiny we have chosen, by not choosing to accept Jesus Christ as our Savior. That is why it is very dangerous to live a perfect trial free life; because we would never be brought to our knees, crying out for God to rescue us, from whatever we may be going through. So, we should thank God for our trials and troubles in this life; for they are the moments that bring us to the humbling places in our lives; so that we may be open to knowing, that we are in dire need of a Savior, Jesus Christ our Lord!

I am sharing my story for three reasons only. First and foremost being: For God's Glory and for His Kingdom; because I feel that God has given me the gift of all these words, and I feel that it is my responsibility to share them with His children for *His Glory*, none other. "I am the vine, you are the branches. He who abides in Me, and I in him, bears much fruit; for without Me you can do nothing." (John 15:5) And second: To help those who may be lost, who may not know that there is a God, an *Almighty God*, that can help us in times of trouble, and that there is *Always Hope*; and that nothing is impossible or too hard for our God! And the third reason is: For people like myself that do know there is a God, and are saved, but may be living without being fed daily – through scripture. For those who may be missing out on what God has created them to do, and the blessings that are awaiting them; which God will reveal to them when they start searching for answers; for answers to questions like: Why they are here? What is their purpose here on this earth? All of these reasons, and all of these thoughts, bring us back full circle, to my saying of: *"From His Glory, For His Glory, None Other."* That is why I am sharing my story – because I feel that the words are *from Him*, and I feel that the words are *for Him*, and that there is just – *no other reason – All is done for His Glory alone!*

So, this is how my search started, and this is what I started doing – I started just asking God: *"What am I supposed to be doing?"* I was just trying to make sense of it all, and thinking to myself – *"There must be something more to life than just doing your same old routines, day after day – from young to old, and then that's it."* Seems so empty, so senseless, so uninspiring – life was so much lacking something; I mean, you can feel it! You can feel down deep inside the longing, that there is more to all of this than just what we are doing here, on this earth. This is what the Bible says about it:

"He has made everything beautiful in its time. Also He has put eternity in their hearts, except that no one can find out the work that God does from beginning to end."
Ecclesiastes 3:11

Jesus Is Who We Are Searching For

Jesus is a real person, a person we can relate to, and who understands us. Jesus is who we are searching for, and He is who we were created for! This is why we all are always searching for something to make us happy; to fill that emptiness or whatever we feel we may be in need of or missing in our lives. It is the relationship with Jesus, and the Hope of Heaven, that we are all searching for. It is the Hope of everything perfect and grand. To be loved unconditionally by the Father that created us. That perfect Friend that will never leave us, the one Friend that will always be with us and for us. The One, that understands us better, than we understand ourselves. Jesus is the Comforter of our soul; He is the One, and the only One, that can make us feel complete and truly loved. Because, you see that is how God created us: *With Eternity in our hearts, and the Hope of Heaven and Jesus being there, and all that, that means.* Jesus is who we are searching for! He is who we desperately need! We just don't realize it at the time. But He does allow things to happen sometimes to get our attention; because if everything was perfect all the time, in our lives, we'd never ever know how badly we need Him! He is the only One that can satisfy that search; because He alone is our perfect desire; He completes us; and He enables us to be our total true selves! We can only find that through Him – Jesus our Lord and Savior – the Friend of all friends!

In the process of my search for God's purpose and His will for my life – life is going on as usual; but, it is at this point, constantly on my mind. I am reading my Bible daily now, and watching my favorite Bible teaching program on Sunday mornings, and then going to church; all the while trusting and waiting for God to show me what He wants me to do next.

The second poem to share would be the second one I had written, when all of this started; this poem was written in the winter of 2016. One winter day back in 2016 – I had been sharing with some friends, a picture of a real snowflake that my daughter had taken with her camera one morning, right after it had been snowing lightly; she had taken this picture with a macro lens. She had captured so much detail of this tiny little snowflake, so perfectly shaped, and everyone was in awe that it was a real snowflake. Later on that night, I had been thinking about how surprised everyone was that this was a real snowflake; then, the next morning the words to this next poem, just started flowing out of me. The original handwritten copy was a little rough; I typed it up and made a few changes to it later on. A gift from God, I believe – the poem and the picture of the snowflake. The timing of getting the picture of this snowflake, before it started to melt, was split second. Do you think this was all in God's plan, or not? This next poem is titled – *A Silent Presence*.

"God's Presence Shown Clearly In the Detail of a Tiny Snowflake"

A Silent Presence

Here you see resting silently, is a tiny snowflake so perfectly.
Amazing it is the perfection you see, so much detail, in awe you must be.
A perfect reflection of God's gracious care, even in the tiniest snowflake it is there!
Oh how He must care and love us so, when even in the smallest of snowflakes it shows!

The snowflakes, they say are all different you see.
Not one are the same, just like you and me!
So, whenever you worry over this and over that!
Or, when all that you hear, is all that is bad!
Remember this snowflake and the detail that it bares,
Know deep down inside that God's Silent Presence is always there!

He is our Shepherd, He will carry us through!

Every step that we take, every thought that we have,
Is to lead us to God's perfect purpose, His perfect plan!
Like this snowflake you see had a journey to take.
To be in this image, just to make us think.

Do you think just by chance or a purpose it played?
To show us all, of God's perfection and Grace?

A hidden message in this snowflake, I think.
Is to open our eyes to all of God's Beauty, God's Grace!

So, remember this snowflake and the detail that it bares,
And always know that God does so very much care!

January 2016

The Framed Snowflake Picture with Poem:

The scripture that I had chosen to go with this poem was:

"For I am about to do something new. See, I have already begun! Do you not see it?"
Isaiah 43:19 Holy Bible NLT

My daughter, on her computer, was able to add my poem to the image of her snowflake, thus creating an awesome combination of the poem with the image of the snowflake altogether; so that you could read the poem while also being able to see the snowflake. I loved the combination of the two so much, that I had the picture of the poem with the snowflake *(pictured previously)* nicely framed, and I hung it on my dining room wall. I had no idea what God had planned after this. I assumed later, that the scripture I had chosen to go on the picture, maybe had something to do with my daughter, and something new maybe that God was going to do in her life – but, I just didn't know what exactly was ahead.

My husband and I were awesomely surprised later on, (after the poem, and the choice of scripture was all done, framed, and hanging on the dining room wall) – that **God had answered a ten year plus long prayer** for our daughter and son-in-law. They had surprised us with the news, that they were finally expecting their first baby. *God is good – Always Good!* And that was good news, and definitely a beginning of something new in their lives! But, God was also up to something else, something new in me; if someone would have told me, ahead of time, what was going to happen in my life, I wouldn't have believed them.

With God's Help Are New Beginnings

As I proceeded on with my daily life's journey, I started getting up early in the morning, so that I could read my Bible and devotionals before I would go to work; that was always my plan to do once I retired. Then I decided that it wasn't a good plan to wait, that I should find a way to fit my daily reading of the Bible in now, because you know, we are not promised tomorrow. So then, we should do today what we want to do – those things that are important to us; and reading the Bible daily, *is very important*, for a healthy spiritual life.

I play the guitar and sing a little, I have done this for many years. I am not a great singer or a great guitar player – but I enjoy it very much, and that's what matters. We should enjoy life, because it goes by really fast! I remember long ago, when I was younger and still living at home, watching and listening to my dad as he would enjoy picking out tunes on his guitar while singing, and my mother singing along with him. I remember wishing back then – wishing that I could pick those tunes out on the guitar like he could; but I could never figure out how to do it. He would just sit there reclined back in his recliner picking out tunes by ear, tunes from an earlier time period of my mother and my dad's younger years, and that always amazed me. I remember at age probably thirteen or so, sitting cross-legged on my bed, trying to pick out the melody to the song *Sunshine On My Shoulders* on an old guitar we had around the house, but I was never successful at getting it; but, all the while, the desire to play the guitar and sing was definitely there.

I have worked through the years trying to teach myself how to play the guitar from books, and also by listening to other people play, and trying to figure out what key they were playing in, and how they were strumming or picking the guitar. But, I never seemed to be able to get past this certain level of playing, which would be – just strumming basic chords, and also a little finger picking.

My husband had bought for me, several years ago, a little hand held recorder that records in high quality, to just play around with. So then, I could use this little recorder when I was playing the guitar and singing different country or gospel songs; then later, you could burn them onto a CD, and share them with family. The recorder, I think, is actually supposed to be used for song writing; so that, when you come up with a newly created song melody, you could record it real quick so that you wouldn't forget what you had created – hmm? But, I had no song writing abilities or any intent to write songs at that time; I just enjoyed playing around with the recorder.

After I had gotten the poem about the snowflake back in 2016 – I remember thinking one day back then, that it might be kind of fun – if I could write a poem based off of the idea behind the snowflake poem, which was that *God's presence is with us always*; and then – if I was able to write the poem, then try to see if I could turn it into a song, just for fun – to see if I would be able to do it. So – with God's help, in just a few minutes, I wrote this next poem. I titled it: *Silent Presence.*

"But Jesus looked at them and said to them, "'With men this is impossible, but with God all things are possible.'"
Matthew 19:26

"I can do all things through Christ who strengthens me."
Philippians 4:13

"God's Snowflake Painted Clouds"

Silent Presence

There is a silent presence, you need only look around.
It's there, just like, you feel the wind.
There is a silent presence, you need only look around.
It's there, just like, you feel the wind.

And when, you see the sky so blue, and when, you see the grass so green.
And when, you feel the rain come down, and when, you see the flowers bloom.
You know it's there, you know it's there, you know it's there.
And when, you see the sun come up and when, you see the day so bright.
And when, you see the moon come out, and when, you see the stars so bright.
You know it's there, you know it's there, you know it's there.

There is a silent presence, you need only look around.
It's there, just like, you feel the wind.
There is a silent presence, you need only look around.
It's there, just like, you feel the wind.

And when, you feel a love so strong, and when, you see a smile so bright.
And when, you feel a hug so warm and when, you want to hold them tight.
You know it's there, you know it's there, you know it's there.
And when, your soul yearns for more and when, you have that empty spot.
And when, you hear the Word of God and then, everything's alright!
You know it's there, you know it's there, you know it's there!
There is a silent presence, you need only look around.
It's there, just like, you feel the wind!

August 27, 2016

"For by Him all things were created that are in heaven and that are on earth, visible and invisible, whether thrones or dominions or principalities of powers. All things were created through Him and for Him."
Colossians 1:16

"God's Beautiful Blue Sky Moon"

Some days after I had written the poem *Silent Presence*, I sat down to try and turn this poem into a song. After a while of working with the words to it, along with the guitar, I finally figured out a chord progression that would match and fit along with the words to the song – I had now created my first real song.

"My Creating Songs, Work Station"

As we all know – this life has many ups and many downs, as we journey throughout our days, which God has given to each of us. So with that being said, as I was living out each of these days that God has given to me on this earth, I would encounter daily struggles, inspiring thoughts, or the devil still trying to antagonize me; as these encounters would happen, words would flow through me. They would usually come in a thought process of words grouped together or a chorus at a time, I guess you could say. Sometimes I would get several poems in one day, and many times I would get them one day, and then the next day, and then the next; usually at very inconvenient times, like taking a shower or trying to get ready for work.

When this first started, I would look for something to write on quickly, an envelope in my purse, or a piece of paper close at hand; anything to write on, that I could get the words down quickly – before I would forget them. Then, I finally bought a journal, and I started carrying it with me all the time. I first started writing the poems down in pencil, in case I may need to erase; then I noticed, that I wasn't really having to change them much, and the pencil would smudge, so then I just started writing them in pen. Then I kind of went through a small stage of, I would get a chorus of words but then I would be a little hesitant to write them down in pen – in case I didn't get the rest of the poem. But over time I learned to just write the chorus down, and then continue to do whatever I had been doing when the words started coming, or just be still, then a few more words would come – wait a second – then a few more; and usually in just a few minutes, I would have the whole poem. Occasionally, there would be a change that I would make to the poems here or there; but for the most part, they are all just how I received them from the beginning. I say received because the Bible says:

"Every good gift and every perfect gift is from above, and comes down from the
Father of lights, with whom there is no variation or shadow of turning."
James 1:17

I believe these poems are definitely a gift from God; because I never set out or planned any of this. I never sat down intentionally to write the poems, except for the one which I had mentioned above; and then, even though I had the thought to write it, the words flowed out effortlessly. I had the desire to write it, but I didn't have to search for the words to write down, if that makes sense. I am sharing this, for God's Glory only. I believe that I am to share my story, to hopefully inspire others, to search for their God given gift; because, according to scripture, I believe we all have been given a glorious gift to be used to glorify Him.

I believe that God has given us all gifts, and that we are all – at some point in our lives – at the stepping stones of His will for us; and that He is eagerly waiting for us to surrender our lives to Him, and ask Him for direction on what to do next. I believe that He has a plan for each and every one of us, to utilize our gifts given by Him, for the Glory of His Kingdom; to draw His people back to Himself, and to cause His children to become thirsty for a relationship with Him. I believe that the plans He has for us, are far greater and more awesome, than we could ever imagine; and I believe that He is just waiting for us to say: *"OK, I'm ready – I've tried it my way, and it's not working – I desperately need You in my life, every day 24/7 – for the rest of my days. Lord, please reveal to me, what Your will is for my life. Reveal to me Lord, why am I here on this earth? What is my purpose, and how do I fit into Your plan for Your Glory and Your Kingdom?"*

In the same day that I wrote the poem – *Silent Presence,* (while dealing with daily struggles, and normal routines of the day), I got the words to this poem – I titled it: *This I Pray.*

This I Pray

Keep my patience long, Lord.
Keep my love strong, Lord.
Keep my path straight, Lord.
This I pray all day, Lord.

Every day I pray, Lord
In You I always trust.
There's just no other way, Lord.
Without You, I'm surely a bust.

So, keep my patience long, Lord.
Keep my love strong, Lord.
Keep my path straight, Lord.
This I pray all day, Lord.

I need You every day, Lord
My strength I find in You.
This is why I pray, Lord.
My strength You surely, will renew.

So, keep my patience long, Lord.
Keep my love strong, Lord.
Keep my path straight, Lord.
This I pray all day, Lord.

Amazing Your love so true, I'm so glad Lord that I found You.
Thankful, I'll always be, for everything Lord, You've done for me.

So, keep my patience long, Lord.
Keep my love strong, Lord.
Keep my path so straight, Lord.
This I pray all day, Lord.

August 27, 2016

"He restores my soul; He leads me in the paths of righteousness For His name's sake."
Psalm 23:3

One summer morning, while trying to get ready for the day, I started getting the words to this next poem. I wasn't really thinking about anything, other than, trying to get ready. I remember as the words started entering my mind, thinking – *"Not now, I have nothing to write on"* – but the chorus, and the subject matter was so important – I remember trotting back and forth between the restroom and my music room (where I had a note pad), and writing down the words as I would get them. This is the poem that I received on that day; I titled it – *God's Word.*

God's Word

Watch out for that devil now, he is an evil soul.
Careful now the steps you take, watch out where you go.
He is an evil spirit you see, that wants to take you down.
He'll trip you up and lie to you, to keep you from that crown.

So, guard your soul, with all your might and read the Word of God.
Then you'll know that God loves you and He'll teach you what is right.
The Truth you see is God's Word, we need it every day.
Without it we are lost, and that devil has his way.

So, Watch out for that devil now, he is an evil soul.
Careful now the steps you take, and watch out where you go.
He is an evil spirit you see, that wants to take you down.
He'll trip you up and lie to you, to keep you from that crown.

So, start each day with a prayer, for God to guide your steps.
And listen to the words He says, and let Him lead you there.
The Book you see is our lead, for a better life.
It is God's guidance and His plan, and there I will abide.

So, Watch out for that devil now, he is an evil soul.
Careful now the steps you take, and watch out where you go.
He is an evil spirit you see, that wants to take you down.
He'll trip you up and lie to you, to keep you from that crown.

September 4, 2016

"Be sober, be vigilant; because your adversary the devil walks about
like a roaring lion, seeking whom he may devour."
1 Peter 5:8

The next morning, again while trying to get ready – while downstairs trying to fix my hair and makeup, I started getting the words to this poem. The only thing that I had to write on was, an envelope in my purse, so that is what I wrote the words to this next poem down on; it is titled – *Heaven's Gates.*

Heaven's Gates

Keep your eyes on Jesus, He's the only way.
Take the road less traveled; He'll guide your steps each day.
Jesus is the stairway, to Heaven's Gates.
Invite Him in to your heart, and there He'll forever stay.

He will never leave you; He'll be with you each day.
He'll help you through your troubles, and you'll be joyful all the way.
In Heaven's Gates He'll lead you, in perfect harmony,
And with Him, He will keep you, for eternity.

So, keep your eyes on Jesus, He's the only way.
Take the road less traveled; He'll guide your steps each day.
Jesus is the stairway, to Heaven's Gates.
Invite Him in to your heart, and there, He'll forever stay.

There'll be no returning, to your old ways.
The joy you'll have, the peace within, you'll never want to trade.
The blessings they will overflow, within your life each day.
I promise you, this is where; you'll always want to stay.

So, keep your eyes on Jesus, He's the only way.
Take the road less traveled. He'll guide your steps each day.
Jesus is the stairway, to Heaven's Gates.
Invite Him in to your heart, and there, He'll forever stay.

So, keep your eyes on Jesus, He's the only way.
Take the road less traveled. He'll guide your steps each day.
Jesus is the stairway, to Heaven's Gates.
Invite Him in to your heart, and there, He'll forever stay.

September 5, 2016

"For there is one God and one Mediator between God and men, the Man Christ Jesus"
1Timothy 2:5

As I am writing, and going through this notebook of poems that I have put together, and adding them into my story, it is an odd feeling to me that I have written all of these poems; but yet an *awe* feeling as well. I don't know exactly how to explain it; it's kind of like I can't believe I wrote them, but yet I did. They all came so quick and effortlessly! It doesn't really seem real to me but yet I am holding this book – that I have put together of all these poems, in finished format printed out on paper, and nicely put into notebook sleeves for safe keeping. Is it a God intervening moment in my life, or is it not? – "In Him also we have obtained an Inheritance, being predestined according to the purpose of Him who works all things according to the counsel of His will." (Ephesians 1:11) The next day I got this poem; I titled it – *Always Hope In Jesus.*

Always Hope In Jesus

There is always, Hope in Jesus.
He truly is our Friend.
Oh He died, on Calvary's Mountain,
Just to free, free us all, from sin.

When you feel, there's no way out, and despair is going to win.
Turn your eyes, to look at Jesus; there is Hope, in Him my friend.
Never give up, on your dreams, never drown in misery.
Take some time, to pray to Jesus, there is power, power in His name.

Yes, there's always, Hope in Jesus.
He truly is our Friend.
Yes He died, on Calvary's Mountain,
Just to free, free us all, from sin.

He will help you, fight the fight; He will keep you, strong indeed.
He will always, be beside you. He is all, you'll ever need.
So, when you feel, like giving up; And you say, I cannot fight.
Just reach up, and call on Jesus. He'll reach down; He'll lift you high.
Just reach up, and call on Jesus, He'll reach down; He'll lift you high.
He'll reach down, He'll lift you high…..

September 6, 2016

"Let us hold fast the confession of our hope without wavering, for He who promised is faithful."
Hebrews 10:23

"The Lord will fight for you, and you shall hold your peace."
Exodus 14:14

A Step By Step Journey of Listening

As you can tell, these poems now sound more like songs. That is because I felt that God had given me all of these words to share with my family and friends. So after I had gotten quite a few of these poems, I started trying to turn them into songs. So what I am sharing, are the poems laid out in chorus and verse formats. So, the choruses are repeated for the purpose of singing them; but, I did not receive them in song pattern. Typically I would get what you see as the chorus, and then the verses would start coming after those first chorus words, if that makes sense. There are additional poems in between some of these dates, written in my small notepad, which I started carrying in my purse. The poems that I am sharing here, in this book, are all of the poems that I have turned into songs, recorded them myself, and then burned them on to CDs. I then created printed CD labels, and also jewel case printed covers for each of the CDs; utilizing either my drawings or pictures that I had taken previously. I also had all of the songs copyrighted with the U.S. Copyright Office. I accomplished all of this, with a lot of prayer, and God's help along the way. And these things did not happen all pre-planned, and as easy as it sounds here; I am just kind of giving an overview of them, as I am thinking of it. It was all very much, just a step by step journey of listening to that soft Voice, and then trying to follow in the way that I felt I was being directed to go. *(Pictured next, are the four CDs featuring, all of the poems/ songs that I am sharing, (**the writings only of them**) in this book.)* All of these tasks were accomplished with Tons of Prayer & God's Help. *("Life Is A Journey" "A Silent Presence" and "Jesus Please" were never turned into songs, and were not added on the CDs.)*

(Written Back In Time © 2017) (I Just Want To Stay © 2020)
(All Around Me © 2021) (Runneth Over © 2022)

This Treasure in Earthen Vessels

Although the poems came very easily to me, I had to work quite hard to turn them into songs; so that I could share them with family and friends. I was also working a full time job during these years. So, I worked on these CDs during evenings and weekends. I guess when God puts something on our hearts – if there is a will – there is a way! There were a few songs that later came along a little easier; I will share that when I get to them; my mother calls those songs *"anointed."*

There are stories in the Bible which tell us about some of God's people that were, either not qualified, or who felt that they were not qualified, to do what God was calling them to do; one of them comes to mind, and that would be Moses. Moses didn't think that he could speak well enough to carry out what God was calling him to do.

I feel, very much not qualified for the task, that I feel God has given me to do; but with His help and His blessings, and if it is His will – I pray that He will enable me to complete the good work, that I feel He has started in me. A lot of the characters that God used for His purposes, in the Bible, were all flawed in some way. You see, we are all broken, and have failed in some way or another but God still loves us, and He still wants to use us for His Kingdom. That is why He created all of us, and that is why we are all here – to *Glorify Him!* No matter how unqualified we may feel, or actually be – I believe that if we are following His will, and on the correct path in which He created us for, that He will enable us – be with us, and bless us on that journey.

It is very interesting to me, when I think back over time – Remember earlier when I had mentioned – when sharing about my earlier guitar playing abilities, and not being able to get past a certain level of playing; which would be basic chord strumming, and a little finger picking. Well, since getting all of these poems, and in my process of trying to turn them into songs, and trying to find a melody on the guitar strings so that my voice would have something to follow; well, this process seems to be helping me to learn more on my guitar, and also developing new ways of playing. Remember I had shared, that I had been trying to progress on the guitar in my earlier years, and was not successful at moving forward with it; I feel like God is now helping me with this, through the poems that He has given to me. It is truly amazing how God works things out, and how He fulfills the desires within us – when we are searching, and trying to follow what His will is for us – What an Awesome God we serve!!!

"For it is the God who commanded light to shine out of darkness, who has shown in our hearts to give the Light of the knowledge of the glory of God in the face of Jesus Christ. But we have this treasure in earthen vessels, that the excellence of the power may be of God and not of us."
2 Corinthians 4:6-7

God's Creation Is So Wonderful To Observe. I titled this one:
"God's Busy Bee"

This next poem came to me in a moment of time, when my mind had gotten off course a little, and back into the senseless worries – that sometimes tries to take hold of us. God always gives us little reminders that He is still here; so never get discouraged, and just keep on looking up to Jesus! This song is titled – *Heaven Will Prevail.*

Heaven Will Prevail

This life soon will pass, Heaven will prevail.
Keep your mind on Jesus stuff.
This life soon will pass, Heaven will prevail.
Keep your mind on Jesus stuff.
You will never fail. You will never fail.

Don't let worries overcome, don't let them be your guide.
For in your life they'll overrun. Don't let worries overcome.
Keep a steady foot ahead, with God's promises instead.
Never waver, never doubt, keep God's word and faith about.

Cause this life soon will pass, Heaven will prevail.
Keep your mind on Jesus stuff.
Yes, this life soon will pass, Heaven will prevail.
Keep your mind on Jesus stuff.
You will never fail. You will never fail.

Things of this life will soon be gone. Things done for Jesus will live on.
So spend your time on things to come, then peace, joy and happiness will overrun.
Things of this life will soon be gone. Things done for Jesus will live on.
So, spend your time on things to come, then peace, joy and happiness will overrun.

September 8, 2016

"For our light affliction, which is but for a moment, is working for us a far more exceeding and eternal weight of glory, while we do not look at the things which are seen, but at the things which are not seen. For the things which are seen are temporary, but the things which are not seen are eternal."
2 Corinthians 4:17-18

God Is a Very Loving and Creative God

You see our God is a very creative God, just look around at all of nature. It is so awesome and limitless in its colors and depths and size of creativity. Stop and look at all of the plants, the trees, and the flowers, and at the wildlife! And just stop, and think – about the love of our puppy dogs. I believe that a puppy dog's love is probably the closest thing we can get, to show an example of God's love for us, here on this earth. Our puppy dog's love is so unconditional! They are so excited to see us when we get home! Whether we were gone for hours, or five minutes – they are always so excited to see us; and they eagerly wait for us to show them some attention and talk to them!

"God's Twinkling In the Love of Our Puppy Dog's Eyes"

That is how God loves us, *unconditionally;* and God is always waiting for us to talk to Him. It's just amazing! God has created this earth, and in all its *Glory* it does shine! Just step out at night, and look up at all the stars and at the moon shining so bright. It's just breathtaking, and it puts into perspective, just how big our God is; but yet so kind, and gentle, and loving in nature. Our God is so awesome! Stop and look at the flowers, the beautiful flowers, and think about the cutest puppy dog you've ever seen, and then, ask yourself – *"What kind of character or personality could create something so wonderful and beautiful?"* These things were all created by our God! This is who our God is; and these are all reflections of His character, His personality, His love, and His love for us. He created these things for Himself, but also for us to enjoy; and also for us to see, and through seeing the things that – God has created, we may – better know Him! Just look around, and you will see for sure the character of "God"; when we take in nature created by our God, we see the character, and the creativity of our God! Who wouldn't want Him as their best Friend? Who wouldn't want Him as their Lord and Savior? God has given us all gifts to use for His Glory; and I so believe that when we allow Him to work through us, He will use us for sure! He will use us to fulfill His purposes on this earth, to Glorify Him and His Kingdom; which will, in return, benefit all of us for eternity. I believe that His creativity will shine through all of us, when we allow Him to enter into our lives, and let His *will* flow though us, and into others lives as well, all for His Glory!

"All things were made through Him, and without Him nothing was made that was made."
John 1:3

"For since the creation of the world His invisible attributes are clearly seen, being understood by the things that are made, even His eternal power and Godhead, so that they are without excuse."
Romans 1:20

"But God demonstrates His own love toward us, in that while we were still sinners, Christ died for us. Much more then, having now been justified by His blood, we shall be saved from wrath through Him. For if when we were enemies we were reconciled to God through the death of His Son, much more, having been reconciled, we shall be saved by His life. And not only that, but we also rejoice in God through our Lord Jesus Christ, through whom we have now received the reconciliation."
Romans 5:8-11

"Then you will call upon Me and go and pray to Me, and I will listen to you. And you will seek Me and find Me, when you search for Me with all your heart."
Jeremiah 29:12-13

(This is another picture, which I have taken; while admiring God's painted skies.)
I titled it:
"God's Amazing Angel Way Up High"

"The heavens declare the glory of God; And the firmament shows His handiwork."
Psalm 19:1

I started getting this next song, again at an inconvenient time. I believe God definitely has a sense of humor! So, I am trying to remember all of these words, as they are entering my mind, thinking to myself – *"remember – remember,"* until I can get something to write them down on before I forget. Too funny! This song is titled: *Joy with Jesus.*

Joy with Jesus

There is Joy with Jesus, There is peace within.
You'll be singing out strong, you'll be dancing freed from sin.
There is Joy with Jesus, Oh the peace you'll feel.
Oh the happiness will flow, from your heart so real.

There is Joy, Joy, Joy with Jesus.
To your heart's content.
There'll be Joy, Joy, Joy with Jesus.
You'll be heaven bound and heaven sent.

There is Joy with Jesus that you can't explain.
You'll just know that it's there, and it rains, rains, rains.
There is Joy with Jesus, oh a love so real.
You'll feel in your heart and oh what a thrill.

There is Joy, Joy, Joy with Jesus.
To your heart's content.
There'll be Joy, Joy, Joy with Jesus.
You'll be heaven bound and heaven sent.

There is Joy, Joy, Joy with Jesus.
To your heart's content.
There'll be Joy, Joy, Joy with Jesus.
You'll be heaven bound and heaven sent.
You'll be heaven bound and heaven sent.

September 12, 2016

"These things I have spoken to you, that My joy may remain in you, and that your joy may be full."
John 15:11

We Can't Plant Weeds in Our Garden

We will only have what we have stored in our minds, to work with, when the devil tries to deceive us. If we have absorbed only the thinking of this world, the devil has and will deceive us. But, if we have absorbed the *Word of God* in our minds and in our hearts, then we will have Scripture, *God's Word living in us*, to defeat the devil; the devil will then flee from us, *for we will then **know**, that we can tell him to get away from us*. Then we will be victorious over his lies! We can't plant weeds in our garden, and then expect for beautiful daffodils, and lilies to grow and bloom there; same is true with our minds, we cannot fill our minds with the thinking of this world, and then expect to live victorious, peaceful, and joyful lives. We have to be proactive and mindful to diligently read, and store up in our minds, the truth of our loving Heavenly Father's beautiful Word – **The Holy Bible**; for this truly is the *Truth*, the *Only Truth*, the *Way* and the *Life*. Knowing what the Bible says, will set us free from the devils trickeries. Then we can live *Victorious, Peaceful, Powerful* and *Joyful* lives, when we have read, and/or heard the Scriptures; so that we may have the Word of God in our hearts and in our minds. And, if we also have the Holy Spirit living within us, the Holy Spirit will help bring up those Scriptures in our hearts and in our minds; all of those Hopes and Promises that God has given to us through His Word; and *He*, the *Holy Spirit,* will remind us of all these things that we have read or have heard in Bible teachings.

With the tools that God has given to us through His word, we will have something to fight with, and we can tell the devil to flee from us when he tries to bring us down, or when he tries to trick us. We will be *Powerful* through *God's Strength* and *His Word,* to stand against the devil's trickery. We will be *Strong* through *God's Love,* to withstand the struggles in this life. We will be *Victorious:* with our *God on our side, Jesus with us,* and the *Holy Spirit living in us!* What a Wonderful, Powerful and Confident way to live!

"Your word I have hidden in my heart, That I might not sin against You."
Psalm 119:11

"Sanctify them by Your truth. Your word is truth."
John 17:17

"Then Jesus said to those Jews who believed Him, 'If you abide in My word, you are My disciples indeed. And you shall know the truth, and the truth will make you free.'"
John 8:31-32

"God's Vibrant Orange Lilies"

The Songs

I, I write the songs, to make the devil, the devil run.
And I, I write the songs, to lift Jesus, Jesus high.
Oh, oh, oh, I, I write the songs, in hopes to help, to help someone,
I ….. I write the songs.

I, I write the songs, to bring you, to bring you joy.
I, I write the songs, to say He, yes He's the One.
Oh, Oh, I, I write the songs, to show you, to show you truth.
I …. I write the songs.

I, I write the songs, to make the devil, the devil run.
And, I, I write the songs, to lift Jesus, Jesus high.
Oh, Oh, Oh, I, I write the songs, in hopes to help, to help someone.
I …. I write the songs.

I, I write the songs, to make the devil, the devil flee.
And I, I write the songs, to say trust, yes trust in Thee.
Oh, Oh, Oh, I, I write the songs, to lead you, to be free.
I …. I write the songs, I …. I write the songs.

September 23, 2016

"Therefore submit to God. Resist the devil and he will flee from you."
James 4:7

Only God Knows All Things

I look back at how this has all happened, and I just kind of shake my head. I am just trying to keep moving forward, and not giving up. Sometimes I get discouraged, and I think to myself – *"Does any of this, that I am doing, even really matter?"* Then I have to remind myself, that I have to just keep on trusting God with all of it; and know in my heart, that God has a plan, and that is all I need to know about it. All I know is that I feel at peace when I am doing what I feel God wants me to do, and that comforts me and satisfies all my questions. So, I just keep on taking that next step that I feel God is calling me to; that is all any of us can do – because, *Only God knows all things.* So, this is how I try to look at it: If the words I am getting, line up with the things that I have read in the Bible, or from Bible teachings, then the words are good words; and they will hopefully benefit God's Kingdom, and fulfill their purpose. That is my hope and my prayer: that if even one person is touched by the songs/poems, or any of these writings, and wants to know Jesus for themselves, and then believes in and trusts in Jesus with their life; and that changes their lives for the better; and their destination changes to their glorious home in Heaven; then, the *angels* will celebrate in Heaven, and all these things will have accomplished their purpose, and were worthwhile time spent!

"So shall My word be that goes forth from My mouth; it shall not return to Me void, But it
shall accomplish what I please, And it shall prosper in the thing for which I sent it."
Isaiah 55:11

"Likewise, I say to you, there is joy in the presence of the angels of God over one sinner who repents."
Luke 15:10

"God's Thunderous Clouds Going Forth"

You Are All I Need

You are all I need; Yes You are all I need.
Thank You, Thank You Jesus, You're all I need.
When this life gets you down, He's all you need.

So, spend some time in Jesus, He will, He'll lift you up.
And when your heart aches and you're down.
Just call on Him, He'll turn it around.
Just call on Him, He'll turn it around.
Never lose heart in things to come.
Always know Jesus is the One.
He's in control of this world you see,
He'll never, no He'll never, just let it be.

Yes, He is all I need; Yes He is all I need.
Thank You, Thank You Jesus, You're all I need.
When this life gets me down, He's all I need.

So when you see things, you just don't understand.
And when, you see things, that just don't seem right.
Always know God's Word does stand,
And that devil, he'll never win the fight.
Greater is He that is in you, than that devil in this world.
So, keep a strong foot on good to do,
And always hold tight, to God's Promises too!

September 12, 2016

"And my God shall supply all your need according to His riches in glory by Christ Jesus."
Philippians 4:19

"You are of God, little children, and have overcome them, because He
who is in you is greater than he who is in the world."
1 John 4:4

For His Glory

Never lose sight of your goals. Never veer off the good path.
Always keep your eyes on Jesus. He will guide you thru His plan.

For His Glory, He will lead you, to His good and righteous plan.
For His Glory, He will lift you, He will lift you, high my friend.

Sometimes, you just don't know how.
Sometimes, you just don't know where.
Sometimes, you just stop and listen.
He will surely guide you there.

For His Glory, He will lead you, to His good and righteous plan.
For His Glory, He will lift you, He will lift you, high my friend.

This is how you know it's Jesus.
This is how, He loves you so.
He just truly wants to bless you.
This is why, I tell you so.

For His Glory, He will lead you, to His good and righteous plan.
For His Glory, He will lift you, He will lift you, high my friend.
For His Glory, He will lift you, He will lift you, high my friend.

September 13, 2016

"Humble yourselves in the sight of the Lord, and He will lift you up."
James 4:10

God Is Our Awesome Healer and Comforter

I believe we all go through different ups and downs in our lives. Some of us have been healthy all of our lives, and some of us have had to deal with a little, and some more than we can bear. But I do strongly believe that everything we go through has purpose; and that God will bring us through it, when we are leaning, and trusting in Him through all of it. His promise is to work all things out for the good for those who love Him and trust in Him. "And we know that all things work together for good to those who love God, to those who are the called according to His purpose." (Romans 8:28)

Just a little history on myself, and a time during my life, when I was having some serious health problems; which involved several years of doctor's appointments, many procedures, and then surgery. Back in the beginning of 1999 I had developed some lung issues. The family doctor thought that it might be walking pneumonia. She treated me with antibiotics for several weeks with repeated X-rays. The antibiotics were not working. I was then referred to a pulmonary doctor who ordered a CT scan, which showed that there may be a tumor in my left lung. So then he ordered a bronchoscopy. The bronchoscopy revealed that I had bronchiectasis, which is an enlarged or widened bronchial tube. During the bronchoscopy they took a culture, which later the results were revealed, and I was diagnosed as having (MAC) Mycobacterium Avium Complex; a lung disease that is very difficult to treat. The doctors had identified this (MAC) in my left lung. The doctor had told me that (MAC) was similar to Tuberculosis; that it was not contagious but was very difficult to treat. I was immediately put on 1000 mg of antibiotics a day for a month. In August of 1999 I started having lung issues again, and was then put back on the antibiotics. This regimen continued through October, November and again in January of 2000.

There was a lot of praying going on through all of this process by my husband, family members, and myself. God is good, and I trust Him! Because you see, with God it is a Win…Win! If He heals us, and we survive whatever is endangering our health – well then, we get to continue living here on this earth, and spreading God's word, and enjoying life. But, if it is His will, to call us Home – Then, *We Get To Go To Heaven!*; where there is *endless Joy*, and *Peace*, and *Life*, and *Pleasures evermore* with our *Lord Jesus Christ, forever and ever.* See, we can't lose! There is so much *Peace* in knowing, that no matter what happens in our lives, God has our back; when we believe in Him, and are trusting in Him!

> "Blessed be the God and Father of our Lord Jesus Christ, the Father of mercies and God of all comfort, who comforts us in all our tribulation, that we may be able to comfort those who are in any trouble, with the comfort with which we ourselves are comforted by God."
> 2 Corinthians 1:3-4

On February 10, 2000 I received a phone call from my pulmonary doctor. He told me he had been to a conference, and that he had learned of a new regimen of medications to try. He wanted me to come in, and see him, and have another CT scan done. So I came in for the appointment, and had another CT scan done; and it revealed that the (MAC) was still in the left lung, and was now slightly moving into the right lung. In addition to that, the doctor said that I was still wheezing in the left lung, and now also slightly in the right lung, as well. On March 8, 2000 the doctor put me on three different antibiotics, for a total of 1900mg of antibiotics a day for a year, with no promises that this was going to clear me of the (MAC); but, very hopeful, that it would. I also had to have routine eye exams, and liver function tests because of the possible side effects from all the antibiotics. I called my Mom, and asked her if she could please put me on the prayer list at her church; I told her that it was very important that I am able to take all of these medications without any side effects; she told me that she would. Thanks to all of the prayers, I was able to take all of the medications with no complications. Thank you Jesus!

In March of 2001, after I had completed a full year of antibiotics, I was taken off all of the antibiotics to see how I would do; within 3 months of being off the antibiotics I started developing lung issues again. More tests were done, and the (MAC) was still there. I remember my Husband telling me that he had been praying so much about this that it has probably turned into pestering. Through all of this time I continued to be on the prayer list at my mother's church, and also my family continued to pray for me as well. We can never ever give up on praying! Worrying not, and praying always! Faith arises when we wait upon the Lord!

"But those who wait on the Lord shall renew their strength; They shall mount up with
wings like eagles, They shall run and not be weary, They shall walk and not faint."
Isaiah 40:31

To bring this story to a conclusion without much more detail, there were many more doctor's appointments, tests and procedures; with still no progress or healing of the (MAC). So, I was then referred to a new infectious disease doctor, which included the continuation of more medications for some time; with end results over time of still testing positive for the (MAC). At this time, I was told by my doctor, that the only hope of eradicating this infection was, to remove the part of the lung that was affected the most; and then continue medications, in hopes of a negative culture report at some point soon.

So, in following my doctor's recommendations, I was referred to a pulmonary surgeon; and on March 18, 2002 I was scheduled to have the lower part of my left lung removed at the Heart Hospital. All of my family was there for me for that surgery; the family support and prayers were very comforting, and I appreciated everyone being there very much! The surgery went very well; the recovery was long and painful. After the surgery, more antibiotics were taken, and more test were done; which revealed to be still positive for the (MAC).

On January 8, 2003 during one of my doctor's appointments, the doctor had told me that we would do another bronchoscopy and culture next month; and then, if we were to get another positive on that test, that he was going to stop trying to cure me of the (MAC); and that the goal going forward would be, to just try to keep the (MAC) stable. The reason being for this he said, was because it was not healthy for me to be on all of these antibiotics for too much longer. So then after this doctor's appointment, I called my mother to update her, and let her know what the doctor had said.

On February 21, 2003, the Friday before I was to go in and have the next bronchoscopy done, my mother called me; she said that she didn't know if it was just her own feelings, or if God was speaking to her. She told me that she kept getting these real strong feelings that she should call me, and see if there was any way that we could come to her church on Sunday, and let the pastor and the people lay hands on me, and pray for me. She wanted to have them lay hands on me, and pray that I may be healed of the (MAC), and pray that we may get a negative result on this next bronchoscopy and culture test. I told her *"yes"* that we could come to her church, and let them pray for me; we definitely needed all the prayers that we could get.

That next Sunday morning, my husband and I got up early, and headed to the church. My mother and my dad were both there, and my aunt was there as well. We were very happy to see them there. The church started the service with singing songs, and worshiping God. I really enjoyed it! The message that morning was about miracles. The pastor delivered a very strong message on how Jesus performed miracles when He was here on earth, and how He is still performing miracles today. He also talked about trusting God in all situations, and also having faith and keeping the faith that God will answer our prayers when we are trusting in Him; and for us to believe that He will answer no matter what one's situation may be.

I stayed pretty emotional off and on that whole morning. When the sermon was over, the invitation started. The song that the worship team played during the invitation was titled, *You Deserve the Glory;* and some of the words to that song were, *You do miracles so great.* This was a very touching song to me that morning, and still is today. I went forward while they were singing that song, and my mother went with me. I told the pastor what was going on with my health issues, and that I was getting ready to have another bronchoscopy done that next morning. I asked him if he would please pray for me, that I would be healed of the (MAC), and pray that we would get a negative on the results of the next culture test. He said, *"He would."* The pastor then told the church what I had told him. Then several people gathered around me, and the pastor anointed me with oil. Then the pastor and the people laid hands on me, and he began to pray; he prayed that I would be healed of the MAC, and that we would get a negative result on the next culture. During the pastor's prayer, he also prayed that my husband and I would see that God is bigger than this problem, and for us to see how important God is. After the pastors prayer I thanked him for praying for me. When I turned around to walk back to my seat, I saw many caring people with watery eyes. Several people gave me a hug after that prayer, and told me that God loved me. This was a very caring and God loving church. It made me feel good to be there, and I also felt at peace there. I returned to my seat, to my husband and my dad, who both also had watery eyes.

The next morning, on February 24, 2003, we got up early and headed to the hospital for my bronchoscopy to be performed and culture taken. After the bronchoscopy was completed, we talked to the doctor, and he told us that if the MAC was still there, it would show up in one month time; but, they were actually going to watch it for two months, just to make sure. He told us that he would call us if, and when anything was to show up on the cultures. Out of all the bronchoscopies that I have had done previously, I always pretty much knew what the results were going to be, by how I was feeling, but this time I wasn't sure. The wheezing that I was hearing and feeling in my lungs previously, I couldn't really hear or feel it anymore; I really felt like something was different this time.

On March 10, 2003 I had a doctor appointment with my pulmonary doctor to go over the pictures that were taken during the bronchoscopy, and to see what the culture was doing at that point of time. He showed us the pictures that he had taken inside of my lungs, in the area where most of the MAC was. He told us that the bad area in my lungs now looked really good. He also told us that, so far the culture had not produced anything yet. We still had over two more weeks to wait, before the one month time frame was reached for the culture's growth process. Always before, the doctor's office would call us within the first month time frame, to tell us bad news. On March 24, 2003 we had reached, the one month point in time on the culture, and no one had called us yet. This was awesome!! On April 7, 2003 I had an appointment with my eye doctor, and he really remarked about how clear the optical nerve looked, and how healthy it looked; he had never told me this before. I told my eye doctor, how I had went to my mother's church to let them lay hands on me, and pray for me to be healed; He said: *"that is good!"* I don't know if he was a God believing person; but, I just had this really strong feeling, that I should share that with him. He would always ask me, during every eye appointment, what was going on with my health issues now, and how I was doing.

I believe that any time that we feel God may be laying it on our hearts, to share with someone what God has done in our lives, then we should act on that, and we should share it. We never know what God is up to, what He is doing, what He has planned, what He may be doing in someone's life; or how something that we may say, or share, may be life changing in someone else's life. That being said, that is why I am sharing my story now; because I feel that is what God wants me to do. He has done something great in my life, and I want people to know that – ***He is a Good and Powerful, Awesomely Wonderful God!!!!***

On April 24 2003, we had reached two months time on the cultures, and we still hadn't received any calls on the results yet. I just really didn't know how to feel – this was great! On April 28, 2003, I had an appointment with my infectious disease doctor, for a follow up to see how things were going, and to see what the plans were going forward. He asked us, *"If we had heard any results on the culture yet?"* We told him, *"No, we hadn't heard anything."* –

(When I say we – that would be me and my husband – he has been a wonderful help, an awesome comforter and caretaker through all of this time. He has never missed a single procedure or doctor's appointment. He has been with me and beside me all the way; I am so thankful for that! **A Great Big Thank You to him – My Husband!!!!** *I just couldn't imagine not having his continual support. You see, God gives us awesome people in our lives! God always knows just what we need; and I am forever grateful for that!!)*

My infectious disease doctor then told us that he hadn't heard anything on the culture either. He told us to wait a minute, and he would go and see if he could find out what the results were. So, we waited in the doctor's office, while he went to check and see what he could find out.

I can't even explain how it felt, while we were waiting for him to return with whatever the results would be. When he did return to the room, he had a smile on his face, and he sat down; then he looked at me and said, *"Are you ready for some good news?"* And I said back to him, *"I am so ready for some good news!"* Then he said to us, *"The results of the cultures were negative!"* I just couldn't believe it! This was so great! I told him of how we had went to my mother's church the day before my bronchoscopy, so that the pastor and the people could lay hands on me, and pray for me that I would be healed, and that we would get a negative result on this culture. The doctor told us, that he has had people tell him that they had been prayed for, after their bronchoscopy; but he said that it seems to make more sense, to pray before the bronchoscopy – then he smiled. He then told me that the normal procedure to treat MAC was that, if you do finally get a negative result – you will then need to continue the antibiotic regimen for one full year, to make certain of no reappearing of the MAC; then he said, but the good news is, that you are already two months into that year.

On August 17, 2003, we returned to my mother's church, so that I could give a testimony of God's healing and the answer to their prayers for me. Six months later, in February of 2004, I was finally taken off of all of the large amounts of antibiotics. I am still under a pulmonary doctor's care for yearly checkups, and mild maintenance medications as a result of the infection; but the infection (MAC) itself – is gone with no signs of any reoccurring problems; and I am feeling great these days!

So now, here I am this day in the year of 2023, writing to share my testimony – that I have been (MAC) free for all these years now, and I am enjoying being freed from that moment of time in my life, so long ago! A big *Thank You* to God, and to all of my doctors for their medical knowledge, their skilled medical procedures, and for their advice on medications; and also to all those who prayed for healing for me; For all these things, truly worked together, in getting me through that time in my life. God is so good and so faithful!

> "Is anyone among you sick? Let him call for the elders of the church, and let them pray over him, anointing him with oil in the name of the Lord. And the prayer of faith will save the sick, and the Lord will raise him up. And if he has committed sins, he will be forgiven."
> James 5:14-15

We Have To Keep Moving Forward

If we are still alive and living on this earth, whether our life has been perfect to date, or if one of us have been through a time in our life similar to what I have previously shared about my health; or possibly there has been something way worse which one has survived, whether it was an accident or an illness or maybe someone is going through something right now. God has a purpose for it, and a purpose for us; something wonderful that He has specifically for us to do. Maybe a wonderful story for us to tell of our testimony, I don't know – but God knows. We all have been given different gifts from God; some may be gifts that we are not even aware of yet. I believe with all my heart that if we will pour out our hearts to God, and ask Him what He wants us to do, what His will is for us; then if we would be still and wait for Him to move, I believe that He will reveal that to us. And I think that we will all be truly amazed at what He will do in our lives for His Glory; if we would just ask.

But I am learning for sure – that we have to keep on taking that next step to move through it. And as we take that step then He reveals the next step. It is truly amazing! We don't get to see it all at once. Just like life, we don't get to see our lives in whole; we live moment by moment. The same is so very true with following what we believe to be God's will for us. If He gives us something to do, or has revealed something to us, if He has laid something on our hearts, even if it is just a little thing – our best response is to just do it. Then just keep on doing the next thing that we feel He is calling us to do. Then one day, we will look back over our days, and we will be thinking – *"huh – So, that's what that was for!"* – *"I wonder what God has for me to do next?"* It is a very exciting way to live our lives. It is definitely becoming more and more noticeable to me that we can't just stop, and we can't give up; even if we have the feelings of – *"Why should I?"* If we don't keep taking that next step – well then, nothing gets done, and we are not moving forward. Then we get down on ourselves because we are not making any progress. Without moving forward and taking that next step, we will never find out what God had for us around that next corner. We just can't give up!

One day I was sitting at our kitchen counter bar with one of my grandson's (at about age five then), and he was playing with a kitchen timer, that I had setting there on the counter. And as he was playing with the timer, just out of the blue, he said – *"Time Is Precious Grandma,"* and I said back to him, *"Yes it is!"* And he is absolutely correct, time is so precious, and it goes by so fast! We are only here on this earth for such a short time, compared to eternity in Heaven. In my heart – I want to make sure that I have accomplished what God created me to do, and I pray that I am on the right path; so, I have to encourage myself to keep taking that next step. I pray that before God calls me home, that I don't disappoint Him, and that I have accomplished all He planned for me to do while I am here on this earth. But that doesn't mean that what God gives us to do should be stressful. I believe that what God has planned for each one of us to do, that we will find *Joy* in it, and *Contentment;* and as He helps us along, and gives us strength – it will be a perfect union of working together, when we are in His will. Because it will be what God has created us to do, the perfect fit for us as individually appointed out by God. I personally feel more alive and motivated when I am in the middle of working on what I feel God has called me to do. I am just saying that sometimes we have to push ourselves to get started, and then the *Joy* fills our souls as we see what God is doing through us. It truly is fulfilling!

"Cause me to hear Your loving kindness in the morning, For in You do I trust; Cause me to know the way in which I should walk, For I lift up my soul to You."
Psalms 143:8

"The steps of a good man are ordered by the Lord, And He delights in his way. Though he fall, he shall not be utterly cast down; For the Lord upholds him with His hand."
Psalms 37:23-24

The Greatest Giver of Gifts

Whatever our gift is – *our God given gift,* whatever it is that God has blessed us with being good at, whatever it is that we thoroughly enjoy doing that is good – we ought to give God the *Glory* for it, and lift God high with it. We should do our best to bless others with our gifts, it could be anything: Some of us might be great comforters or encouragers; some may be good at fixing things, or a good mechanic, or capable of restoring things to new again; maybe it is art, or music that we love; it could be photography, or any kind of indoor or outdoor sports. God is the creator of all things, and the giver of our gifts. We all have something in our hearts that we love to do. I believe that when we *Glorify God* and give Him the credit for it, that He blesses us in whatever we are doing, when our goal is to do it for *His Glory – that He may be high and lifted up.*

Another gift that I truly believe that God has given to each of us, and that is the gift of giving. The Bible says that we were created in His image, and God is the greatest giver of gifts, that there can be or ever will be. He gave us the *Gift* of *His Son, Jesus Christ,* to die for our sins; that if we believe in Him – we shall be saved, and have Eternal Life. We celebrate this awesome gift of Jesus every Christmas. I am so thankful for the Christmas Season – so that we may be reminded each year of this awesome gift of *Jesus!*

> "For God so loved the world that He gave His only begotten Son, that whoever
> believes in Him should not perish but have everlasting life."
> John 3:16

Sometimes we receive gifts that have the ability to stir our emotions – like the gift of Jesus! When we really understand what Jesus means to us, it will stir the *Joy* in us, quite much! With that in mind – One previous Christmas, I had received a wonderfully awesome Christmas gift, *one that I will cherish always!* – It was a beautiful battery operated snow globe lantern. The lantern was finished in a bronze colored top and bottom frame, with a clear area in the center. There within the center of the globe was the Nativity Scene of Jesus, *baby Jesus* with Joseph and Mary. The snow globe lantern had a light illuminating in it, with a little hidden fan blowing small pieces of glitter all around; simulating glistening snowflakes floating softly around the *baby Jesus* in the manger. In the evening with the lights down low, and that lantern on, it was beautiful – breathtaking to me. It just was so calming and peaceful as I would watch the sparkle of the simulated snow illuminating – as if it were night time and the moon was giving the snow its gleam. I wanted to give a gift back in return, for what had been given to me; but I just could not come up with anything that even came close, to the gift that I had received. As I thought on this, for some time it seemed like – I started getting all of these words. I believe that the words were a gift from the Holy Spirit to me, to give back as a gift in return. As

I began to write all of these words down, they seemed to all fall together on the paper – so similar to me, as to the glitter floating around in the lantern, with the *baby Jesus* in the nativity scene. When I was done writing, and read the finished poem – I felt that God now had given to me, that special gift that I was searching for. I was so grateful for the poem, and I was excited now to give my gift back in return; I typed up the poem, printed it, and put it in a frame, and then presented my gift – as what I hoped would be a blessing in return.

"Every good gift and every perfect gift is from above, and comes down from the
Father of lights, with whom there is no variation or shadow of turning."
James 1:17

"As each one has received a gift, minister it to one another, as good stewards of the manifold grace of God."
1 Peter 4:10

I am sharing now the words to that poem; I have changed only the title of the poem, for the purpose of this book. I have title it: *The Gifts That You've Given.* I pray God's blessings on it, and on the reader of it.

"Oh, taste and see that the Lord is good; Blessed is the man who trusts in Him!"
Psalm 34:8

The Gifts That You've Given

The gifts that you've given are priceless indeed!
So, I thought, what could I give...
that would be as precious as these.
So, I thought & I thought and nothing compared.
To the awe that I felt......
as the snow danced around in the glistening light,
surrounding the Baby Jesus as He slept in the night.
So as I thought & I thought all these words of
gratitude did surely come.
So I decided I could write them down
as I received them one by one.
So here is my gift from me to you,
in appreciation of the kind things that you do.
As we watch the simulation of the snow....
glistening in the light.
As the sparkles in the light do dance in the bright.
I pray God's Blessings on the Kindness you've shown.
And May God Bless you in return
for your blessings bestowed.

Sherri L. Land

December 2020

All Have a Greater Purpose

It is truly interesting to me, how some things happen in our life that seem to be so random, and just the happenings in the day, with not much purpose for it – other than just enjoying whatever that might be. I know that sounds like kind of a long sentence but this is how one of my days started – just random.

Several years ago we used to have a bird feeder out in the back yard, and we would keep black oil sunflower seeds in it. The birds and the squirrels would get kind of messy while eating, and in the process, some of the whole sunflower seeds would fall on the ground. This particular summer, one of the seeds had sprouted, and had grown a few inches. When I saw that the sunflower plant already had a pretty good growth start, I had just casually mentioned to my husband – *"That maybe we don't mow this one down. That I would like to just let this sunflower grow."* I thought it would be fun to watch its growth process; so, we both decided to let it grow.

"God's Early Morning Sun Rising Follower"

I had so much fun watching all of the changes that the sunflower went through that summer. The first thing I noticed, which I should have already known, but I had never observed a sunflower as closely as I did this particular summer; but, what I noticed, was that it follows the sun from morning to evening… so cool! I started taking pictures every day of this sunflower. I felt that the sunflower resembled how we should live our lives, following the *Son (Jesus)* from morning to night. It was quite amazing and very dramatic, the movements that it would make throughout the day. The bloom would start out in the morning facing directly extreme east, by evening it would be facing directly, and extreme to the west. Then when I would get up in the morning it was facing directly and extreme east again. I know that all flowers do this to some degree – but the sunflower just seemed to be so much more dramatic.

The other observation I noticed while watching, and taking pictures of the sunflower was, all the changes it went through; truly fascinating! I don't know for sure but I would guess that the sunflower probably goes through more changes than any other flowering plant. It also reminded me of us, as children of God, and all the changes that we go through, as we are growing into the person that God created us to be. It was quite a process this sunflower went through, all of its natural changes, all the while following the sun. It seemed very symbolic to me, of all the changes we go through, and how we grow spiritually as we are reading our Bibles and devotionals, while trying to follow the *Son (Our Lord Jesus Christ),* the best that we can. We change and grow spiritually following the *Son,* just like the sunflower is growing, and changing in nature following the sun. So very wonderful and educational, nature is to observe!

"God's Beautiful Sun Follower, Awakening, Just a Few More Petals to Go"

At the same time that I was observing, and taking pictures of this sunflower, I was also working on my second CD, titled: *I Just Want To Stay.* I had been trying to come up with an idea for the image that would go on the cover of this CD. I kept thinking that I was supposed to try to draw a flower, and make that the image for the cover. But I couldn't figure out which flower I should try to draw, and I didn't really feel like I could draw a flower like what I wanted. By the time I was close to finishing the CD, at the point where I now needed the cover idea, it was turning to fall, and all of the flowers were now dying; so, I couldn't even try to take a picture of a real flower, and use it. I was becoming very discouraged with not having the image that I needed.

Then one morning, while I was fixing my breakfast, I started hearing this soft *Voice* telling me, *"You already have taken the perfect picture for the cover of your CD – the sunflower picture, with the honeybee on it."*

Because you see, I had already gotten the words that I was going to add on the inside of this second CD cover, (I have entered on the inside of each of my CD covers, inspirational words that I believed at that time God wanted me to insert therein; pertaining to whatever the subject matter might have been, on that particular CD). So, those words that I had gotten previously for this second CD, were talking about staying focused on God's Word, like the honeybee is focused on getting nectar. In addition, I was also already planning to use a picture of a honeybee on a balloon flower, which I had previously taken; I was going to use this image on the inside of the CD cover. So, the picture of the sunflower with the honeybee on it was actually just exactly what I needed, and it fit right in with all that was already going on, and being talked about within the CD. I was super excited to now have the image for the cover of this second CD. I felt like the *Holy Spirit* had now pointed me in the direction I was to go, and leading me to the picture I was to use now for the second CD cover. I had not taken any of these pictures of the sunflower, or of the balloon flowers with any intent to use them for any CD idea at the time. I was just enjoying watching the sunflower grow. But I do feel now, that God had a purpose for it, all along; and I see now, why I was getting to enjoy the sunflower, as I did. It had a great purpose! Pictured next is the image that I used for the cover of my second CD.

"God's Perfect Example of Survival, Shown Clearly In Nature"

It is truly amazing, how much there is to learn from nature, that we can apply to our own lives. Just like the honeybee needs the nectar from God's sunflower to survive; we so need God's Word to feed on, so that we may know *who God is*, know that *Jesus is His Son*, and know that *Jesus is Alive*. When we are able to feed our souls spiritually with the truths of Scripture and of the Gospels, this truth sets us free, and leads us to our survival – *Eternal Life*. This truth nurtures us, so that we may grow and mature spiritually, and be transformed into the beautiful people God created us to be. Just like our bodies need food to survive, and be healthy – we also desperately need *Scripture (God's Word)* to be spiritually healthy. Then we can be *Loving, Joyous, Peaceful, Patient*, and *Compassionate* people; living *Victorious* lives in this world, and telling others the *Good News of Jesus*.

"Early Morning Sunflower Kissed by God's Rain"

While watching the sunflower, I learned the similarities between children of God, and the sunflower. The *sunflower* – needs the *sun* or it will not grow and it will eventually die. *God's children* – need the *"Son" (Jesus)*, or we can't spiritually grow, and we die spiritually, and are permanently separated from God.

"Jesus said to him, 'I am the way, the truth, and the life. No one comes to the Father except through Me.'"
John 14:6

All the while, just enjoying watching the sunflower's growth process, and thinking that was all I was doing; but, there was so much more going on, and so much more to it. In addition to the things that God was opening my eyes to, while watching the sunflower – God also gave me a story, and also the picture I needed for my CD cover. I had no intent of anything coming out of this experience and time in my life, or were there any particular reason of why I was taking the pictures, or any idea that I would have a story to share out of it; I was simply enjoying God's creation. But, I do feel that God allowed me to enjoy these moments in time for His Glory, and for His purposes. I am very thankful for this experience, and also for the gifts of the images, and for the story which I now have to share from that one summer, as well as, for those moments of enjoying and observing one of God's wonderful creations – the beautiful *Sunflower*.

I guess my take from this experience would be, don't miss our moments; don't take whatever is happening today, and think that it doesn't matter. All of our days, and all of our moments, they all have a greater purpose! All things point to – *"We need the Lord Jesus"* so badly! We have to find ways to live our lives with eyes opened to see, and then God will lead the way.

The following scripture was written by Paul in the year of A.D. 56, it is located in 1 Corinthians:

"For I delivered to you first of all that which I also received: that Christ died for our sins according to the Scriptures, and that He was buried, and that He rose again the third day according to the Scriptures, and that He was seen by Cephas, then by the twelve. After that He was seen by over five hundred brethren at once, of whom the greater part remain to the present, but some have fallen asleep. After that He was seen by James, then by all the apostles. Then last of all He was seen by me also, as by one born out of due time."

1 Corinthians 15:3-8

*"Jesus is **Alive** and All of Nature Shines Brightly with This Truth"*

I am listing throughout the balance of this book, the rest of the *Poems/Songs* that I had received. I will be entering them in the order of the date by which they were written. There were additional poems written between these dates; these are just the ones that I had turned into songs. As I would be working on turning the poems into songs, I would get new poems that I wanted to share as well – thus, creating some gaps in the dates.

I pray that whoever reads these writings – will be blessed by my testimony. *I believe* one hundred percent – that *Jesus is very much ALIVE*, and that *He is, wanting and willing*, to work through us; if we will just *invite Him into our lives.*

I Just Want To Stay

I just want to stay and pray all the day, there is comfort there I say.
And all Your promises, I love them too. I'm so thankful I found You.
We need You, Lord we really do. This world, wants to drag us away from You.
So, we must hold tight and never let go. And always know You love us so.

There is comfort in Your words.
I hold them close to me each day.
I write them down and tuck them away.
They are the stronghold for my ways.

So, I just want to stay and pray all the day, there is comfort there I say.
And all Your promises, I love them too. I'm so thankful I found You.
We need You, Lord we really do. This world, wants to drag us away from You.
So, we must hold tight and never let go. And always know You love us so.

The world and the devil like to say You're not You,
But just look around we know that's not true.
The beauty created just by Your hand,
Is truly proof that Your word stands.

So, I just want to stay and pray all the day, there is comfort there I say.
And all Your promises, I love them too. I'm so thankful I found You.
We need You, Lord we really do. This world, wants to drag us away from You.
So, we must hold tight and never let go. And always know You love us so.

Hearts and lives broke and torn down.
The miracles You bring turn them around.
So much to gain to believe that You're true.
Troubles and trials You turn to good.
Oh to trust Jesus our lives made new.
Oh, to trust Jesus our lives made new.

September 14, 2016

"Peace I leave with you, My peace I give to you; not as the world gives do I give
to you. Let not your heart be troubled, neither let it be afraid."
John 14:27

"Come and see the works of God; He is awesome in His doing toward the sons of men."
Psalm 66:5

He Is Faithful

Jesus, yes He truly loves us. He is faithful too my friend.
He just wants to truly bless you!
Read His Word, you'll find within. Read His Word, you'll find within.

Jesus, He will help you.
He will free you from your sin; He will break away those chains.
He will let you live again. He will let you live again.
Precious Jesus, Thank you Jesus…
On that cross Your blood was shed, Precious Jesus, Thank you Jesus.
Because You live, We too will live. Because You live, We too will live.

Jesus, yes He truly loves us. He is faithful too my friend.
He just wants to truly bless you!
Read His Word, you'll find within. Read His Word, you'll find within.

Thank you Jesus, death has lost.
Because our Father sent You here, Oh my Jesus, Thank you Jesus!
We have nothing left to fear… We have nothing left to fear!
We have nothing left to fear!
Jesus, yes He truly loves us…

September 14, 2016

"Therefore know that the Lord your God, He is God, the faithful God who keeps covenant and mercy for a thousand generations with those who love Him and keep His commandments."
Deuteronomy 7:9

"If we confess our sins, He is faithful and just to forgive us our sins and to cleanse us from all unrighteousness."
1 John 1:9

"A little while longer and the world will see Me no more, but you will see Me. Because I live, you will live also."
John 14:19

Some Quiet Time And Ears To Listen

One morning while on a trip to go see family as we were traveling down the turnpike, I started getting all of these words really fast. Thank goodness I had my journal in my purse – so I pulled it out, opened it up, and proceeded to write the words down as fast as they were entering my mind. The words seemed to be very firm, and very clear – as to be very directive to me. This was one of those poems that seemed to have an anointed melody already equipped along with the words. I believe that God is always trying to communicate with us; but we need to have some quiet time and ears to listen, so that we don't miss what He is trying to tell us. I was very excited about this poem after I finished writing it, and read through it. I believe that it was a message to me, or you might say directions to me, from God. I think that the more we surround ourselves with His Scripture, songs about Him, as well as enjoying His Creation – then the better we can hear what He is trying to tell us. And I believe that it probably always starts with, *"I love you – you are my child, and this is why I tell you so – to protect you."* Just like our earthly parents warn us of things – because they love us, and they want to protect us. I titled this song, *Surround Ourselves.* I pray that you will be blessed by these words that I feel God gave to me, on that day while rolling down the turnpike, and traveling through the Flint Hills of Kansas.

"Vibrant Colors of Pink & Green Beauty In Nature Is Serene"

Surround Ourselves

We need to read the Bible, so we know what God says.
And we need to read the Bible, so we know who He is.
And we need to read the Bible, so we can fight the fight.
And we need to read the Bible, so we know what's right.

We've got to get into God's Word, to hear God's Word.
We've got to surround ourselves with His Love, for Him to Shine.
The world is the clutter in our lives,
We've got to let go for the good to thrive.
Quiet time is needed to hear His whispers,
But we've got to want to hear to recognize.
We've got to seek and then we'll find.
Then in our lives' He will refine.

Yes... We need to read the Bible, so we know what God says.
And we need to read the Bible, so we know who He is.
And we need to read the Bible, so we can fight the fight.
And we need to read the Bible, so we know what's right.

We've got to want the good to override.
And we've got to want the bad to take a ride.
Then we'll want to let our light shine.
Then in your life Christ will be your guide.
And in your life Joy will surely flow,
And from your life the dark will go...go...go...
For in your life the devil is done,
And for your life Christ has won.
AND FOR YOUR LIFE CHRIST HAS WON...

September 20, 2016

"For the word of God is living and powerful, and sharper than any two edged sword, piercing even to the division of soul and spirit, and of joints and marrow, and is a discerner of the thoughts and intents of the heart."
Hebrews 4:12

"In the beginning was the Word, and the Word was with God, and the Word was God."
John 1:1

"As newborn babes, desire the pure milk of the word, that you may grow thereby, if indeed you have tasted that the Lord is gracious."
1Peter 2:2

Things Real and True

Don't let me waste… Don't let me waste…
Don't let me waste… Don't let me waste…
A single day… on something not for You,
Lord help me keep my time spent on things real and true.
Lord help me help those that are in need of You.

Thank you Lord for not giving up on me…
And thank you Lord for your Grace for me to see.
Jesus you are everything to me…
Thank you Lord, for pulling me to shore…
I love you Lord, and I'm grateful evermore…
So Thank You Lord… for in You, I found me.

Don't let me waste… Don't let me waste…
Don't let me waste… Don't let me waste…
A single day… on something not for You,
Lord help me keep my time spent on things real and true.
Lord help me help those that are in need of You.

Jesus is my refuge… and thru Him, I am free.
He has broken every chain… forever grateful I'll always be.
He can do the same for you as He's done for me.
All you have to do… is ask… and then believe.
All you have to do… is ask… and then believe.

September 21, 2016

"Finally, brethren, whatever things are true, whatever things are noble, whatever things are just, whatever things are pure, whatever things are lovely, whatever things are of good report, if there is any virtue and if there is anything praiseworthy – meditate on these things."
Philippians 4:8

"For the Son of Man has come to save that which was lost. What do you think? If a man has a hundred sheep, and one of them goes astray, does he not leave the ninety-nine and go to the mountains to seek the one that is straying?"
Matthew 18:11-12

Thank You Jesus

Thank you Jesus for Your Grace…
You so freely give…
And thank you Jesus…
It's Your desire… for all to live…

We know the price that You have paid, for us all, that we might be saved.
You gave it all, You paid our debt; for our sins Lord, we all regret.
Where would we be… without You Lord; Oh how lost we'd surely be.
Oh on that cross You paid it all, for our sins, Lord; You set us free.

So, Thank you Jesus for Your Grace…
You so freely give…
And thank you Jesus…
It's Your desire… for all to live…

There's now no time for us to waste; for the risk is way too high.
Oh there are folks now needing saved; and there's Jesus to raise high.
What a glorious day Oh it will be; when we meet You in the sky.
And You take us home to be; in that sweet, sweet by and by.

So, Thank you Jesus for Your Grace…
You so freely give…
And thank you Jesus…
It's Your desire… for all to live…

September 21, 2016

"For by grace you have been saved through faith, and that not of yourselves; it is the gift of God."
Ephesians 2:8

"Who Himself bore our sins in His own body on the tree, that we, having died to sins, might live for righteousness – by whose stripes you were healed. For you were like sheep going astray, but have now returned to the Shepherd and Overseer of your souls."
1 Peter 2:24-25

"Whereas you do not know what will happen tomorrow. For what is your life? It is even a vapor that appears for a little time and then vanishes away."
James 4:14

An Awesome Representation

One morning, back in September of 2022, I had decided to go out and tend to my flower garden some; it was in need of a little care. So while I was outside in the backyard trimming my flowers and weeding my small flower garden, just enjoying being outside and enjoying my flowers – when out of the blue, this beautiful large monarch butterfly showed up, to visit some of the flowers, which were growing there. I was in awe! When I saw the butterfly – I could hardly believe what I was seeing, and I was so excited! I went inside to get my phone so that I could take some pictures. I was so afraid that the butterfly would probably be gone when I got back, but it would definitely be worth the chance, if it was still there when I returned. I was very thankful that I did go get my phone because the butterfly was still there among the flowers. It was a wonderful experience; the butterfly just kept fluttering around – all around me, and all around the flowers. The butterfly stayed there visiting the flowers, while I was right there in the midst of the flowers, for some time it seemed like. I was able to take many pictures, and a few videos of this beautiful butterfly created by God.

When we observe nature, I think that God reveals some spiritual secrets to us. The monarch butterfly is an awesome representation of how God transforms something lowly into something beautiful, and gives it wonderful freedom; from a caterpillar crawling on the ground, and on the trees – to freedom of flight. It is wonderfully spectacular! Shown next is my favorite picture, out of all of the pictures that I was able to take on that awesome September day. I was very grateful to have gotten to experience that moment in my life. And very thankful that God had given to me this wonderful, one on one time, with this beautiful monarch butterfly which He had created. It was so awesome to watch this butterfly from such a close range for so long – to get to observe its beautiful colors, delicate wings, and such graceful flight and fluttering patterns – as it worked its way through and around all of the flowers.

I was curious just now – as I am remembering that wonderful experience with the butterfly, and as I am writing this, as to how long the butterfly was actually with me amongst the flowers. So, I just checked my images on my phone to see what time I actually took the first picture, to the time when the last picture was taken. The first picture was taken at 10:17 am, and the last picture was taken at 10:25 am; so I got to be with that monarch butterfly for 8 minutes, and I took seventy-five images (a few of them videos) during that time. God is good – Always good!!

"God's Beautiful Example of Transformation in Nature"

How He Makes Us Strong

Oh when the pressure's on. And things go way too wrong.
That's when we seem to need Him most. That's when we seem to need Him most.
But this is what we surely know; That this is how He makes us strong.
But this is what we surely know; That this is how He makes us strong.

The troubles we endure are only for our good.
Because without them, we'd surely never know, that we need Him so.
When something in your life; brings you to your knees.
You raise your hands up high and pray "Oh Lord Please."

Oh when the pressure's on. And things go way too wrong.
That's when we seem to need Him most. That's when we seem to need Him most.
But this is what we surely know; That this is how He makes us strong.
But this is what we surely know; That this is how He makes us strong.

Oh He is faithful. He is listening. He truly loves us so.
It's when we see our prayers be answered, that our faith does surely grow.
So, thank Him when those times come. Thank Him when the day is done.
So thank Him when days are bright. And thank Him when the pressure's on.

Oh when the pressure's on. And things go way too wrong.
That's when we seem to need Him most. That's when we seem to need Him most.
But this is what we surely know; That this is how He makes us strong.
But this is what we surely know; That this is how He makes us strong.
But this is what we surely know; That this is how He makes us strong.

September 23, 2016

"My brethren, count it all joy when you fall into various trials, knowing that the testing of your faith produces patience. But let patience have its perfect work, that you may be perfect and complete, lacking nothing."
James 1:2-4

"Call upon Me in the day of trouble; I will deliver you, and you shall glorify Me."
Psalm 50:15

Become Spiritually Strong

The devil can be very persistent, but the more knowledge we gain of what the Bible says, and how we can fight these spiritual battles, the stronger we become; and the less frequent we are under attack or it will seem that way anyhow; for we are way less vulnerable when we know the truth. When we know God is on our side, and we have *His Word* in our heart, it changes everything! As we become spiritually strong, the devil loses his power over us! When we know that the devil is a liar, we can tell the devil to *"Just get away from us, we have Jesus now"* – it is a wonderful power, and the devil **will** flee from us! This next poem that I have written titled, *I have Jesus Now* – came to me very fast one morning while being under attack by the devil's tactics again. I had feelings of complete peace over me after I finished writing this poem. God has an awesome way of watching over us, and filling us with *His Peace, His Presence,* and with the *Comfort of His Protection,* when we are *trusting in Him.*

I Have Jesus Now

Get away from me you devil… I am tired of your games.
Let me be to live my life without any more pain.
Your tricks and your trickeries they won't work on me no more.
Because I have Jesus now and He already knows the score.

So don't taunt and tatter any longer. You're not welcome here no more.
Just go away and don't come back. I've tightly shut the door.
The troubles here will soon be gone, because Jesus He has my back.
The Bible surely tells me so; So I won't have no more of that.

Get away from me you devil… I am tired of your games.
Let me be to live my life without any more pain.
Your tricks and your trickeries they won't work on me no more.
Because I have Jesus now and He already knows the score.

We have to put on our fighting gear, so we can fight the fight.
The dark will surely go away; God's Word will be our light.
So don't let that devil drag you down. He, he has no power here.
Just say to him in Jesus name… you… be gone from here.
Yes there's power in Jesus name.

September 23, 2016

"Put on the whole armor of God, that you may be able to stand against the wiles of the devil. For we do not wrestle against flesh and blood, but against principalities, against powers, against the rulers of the darkness of this age, against spiritual hosts of wickedness in the heavenly places."
Ephesians 6:11-12

"Behold, I give you the authority to trample on serpents and scorpions, and over all the power of the enemy, and nothing shall by any means hurt you."
Luke 10:19

Pick Up That Cross

Lay down our lives, pick up that cross.
Jesus Christ…. has paid the cost,
Nothing left… for us to do… but follow Him.

He knows the way and it is good; His plans for us, to follow through.
Pick up that cross and follow Him; Don't lose our souls, and fall away.
He has a plan, and it is good. He knows the way… it's understood.
There's nothing worth… in this world… the cost to stray away.

Lay down our lives, pick up that cross.
Jesus Christ…. has paid the cost,
Nothing left… for us to do… but follow Him.

Jesus never leaves our side. He's the One we can confide.   .
He's the only One that is true. And He surely loves you.

Lay down our lives, pick up that cross.
Jesus Christ…. has paid the cost,
Nothing left… for us to do… but follow Him.

I ask you all to testify… in your lives He has supplied.
For this fight He has won, and His will is surely done.
When time has come… and He has called.
We'll be so thankful… We picked up… that cross,
As He carries us home.

Lay down our lives, pick up that cross.
Jesus Christ…. has paid the cost,
Nothing left… for us to do… but follow Him.

September 25, 2016

"Then Jesus said to His disciples, 'If anyone desires to come after Me, let him deny himself, and take up his cross, and follow Me. For whoever desires to save his life will lose it, but whoever loses his life for My sake will find it. For what profit is it to a man if he gains the whole world, and loses his own soul? Or what will a man give in exchange for his soul?'"

Matthew 16:24-26

Forever On That Cross

Leave your troubles at the feet of Jesus
Lean Forever On that Cross.
Oh your burdens, yes they will leave you…
When you're leaning on that Cross.

Oh never be discouraged…
Oh with Jesus, we are free.
Yes, He has broken all chains among us.
He has set the captive free.

So, leave your troubles at the feet of Jesus
Lean Forever On that Cross.
Oh your burdens, yes they will leave you…
When you're leaning on that Cross.

Oh Troubles, yes they surround us…
In this old world.
Oh but when you have Jesus…
Oh those worries, they have no hold.

So, leave your troubles at the feet of Jesus
Lean Forever On that Cross.
Oh your burdens, yes they will leave you…
When you're leaning on that Cross.

Oh friend… no don't wait. Put your trust in Him today.
Oh He is Faithful… He will brighten… all your days.

So, leave your troubles at the feet of Jesus
Lean Forever On that Cross.
Oh your burdens, yes they will leave you…
When you're leaning on that Cross.

On that Cross... On that Cross.

October 14, 2016

"I have been crucified with Christ; it is no longer I who live, but Christ lives in me; and the life which I now live in the flesh I live by faith in the Son of God, who loved me and gave Himself for me."
Galatians 2:20

"He only is my rock and my salvation; He is my defense; I shall not be moved."
Psalm 62:6

Create A Drive Within Me

Create a drive within me that I cannot stop.
To do Your will, and shout Your name from the mountain top.
Let Your blessings flow like the rains come down.
Cause me to be humble, help me earn that crown.

The love You give is so divine. Let Your living waters quench the thirst we so desire.
Let my eyes see the beauty that Your hands create, let me never forget the price Jesus paid.
Stir a drive within me, to read Your Word, a drive Lord to read it through and through.
Help me understand all Your Words so clear, and please grant me wisdom which is so dear.

Create a drive within me that I cannot stop.
To do Your will, and shout Your name from the mountain top.
Let Your blessings flow like the rains come down.
Cause me to be humble, help me earn that crown.

Lord, help me not to stumble as I walk this earth, I want to be true to the heart of You.
Lord, help me not to give a bad review, that would reflect in any way bad on You.
Lord, help me be the light that You say to see, and help me be the salt of the earth to be.
Lord, keep my steps steady straight in front of me, and please be the light always leading me.
Yes, please be the light always leading me!

October 17, 2016

"I have fought the good fight, I have finished the race, I have kept the faith. Finally, there is laid up for me the crown of righteousness, which the Lord, the righteous Judge, will give to me on that Day, and not to me only but also to all who have loved His appearing."
2 Timothy 4:7-8

"You are the salt of the earth; but if the salt loses its flavor, how shall it be seasoned? It is then good for nothing but to be thrown out and trampled underfoot by men. You are the light of the world. A city that is set on a hill cannot be hidden."
Matthew 5:13-14

"Let your light so shine before men, that they may see your good works and glorify your Father in heaven."
Matthew 5:16

"On the last day, that great day of the feast, Jesus stood and cried out, saying, 'If anyone thirsts, let him come to Me and drink. He who believes in Me, as the Scripture has said, out of his heart will flow rivers of living water.'"
John 7:37-38

Palm of God's Hand

The mountains are high… the valleys are low.
God created them all… Lord it's quite a show.
The flowers in bloom, the trees are so tall. The ocean as wide as you can go.
All held in the palm of God's hand… you know.

The birds of all kinds and the fish in the sea; Yes God created all of these.
Oh I see those birds oh how they fly… so, so high up in the sky.
Oh I hear them sing oh how they sing… Oh how do you explain… all these things?

The mountains are high… the valleys are low.
God created them all… Lord it's quite a show.
The flowers in bloom, the trees are so tall. The ocean as wide as you can go.
All held in the palm of God's hand… you know.

My eyes are brown and yours are blue. I breathe in air and so do you.
God created me… and He created you. And He has a mission for us all to do.
In this big beautiful world… With skies of blue.

The mountains are high… the valleys are low.
God created them all… Lord it's quite a show.
The flowers in bloom, the trees are so tall. The ocean as wide as you can go.
All held in the palm of God's hand… you know.

To love one another it… is a must. Yes we should love others as, He loves us.
And follow His will, as we trust… One step at a time… Led by His light.
Because we follow by faith… And not by sight.

November 20, 2016

"For the Lord is the great God, And the great King above all gods. In His hand are the deep places of the earth; The heights of the hills are His also. The sea is His, for He made it; And His hands formed the dry land. Oh come, let us worship and bow down; Let us kneel before the Lord our Maker. For He is our God, And we are the people of His pasture, And the sheep of His hand. Today if you will hear His voice;"
Psalm 95:3-7

"A new commandment I give to you, that you love one another; as I have loved you, that you also love one another. By this all will know that you are My disciples, if you have love for one another."
John 13:34-35

Runneth Over

Oh Lord fill me with Your joy... Joy that I can't contain;
Oh Lord, let my cup runneth over, like it pours when it rains.
Like it pours when it rains.

Let me be content in all You give... A joy that overflows within;
A heart that shines for all to see; For Your glory the joy will be.
Lord give me peace that fills my heart so. So much that it surely shows.
Oh that It's You Lord that gives peace divine.
For only You Lord, my light will shine... do, do, do, do.

Oh Lord fill me with Your joy... Joy that I can't contain;
Oh Lord, let my cup runneth over, like it pours when it rains.
Like it pours when it rains.

Lord, give me love that radiates; Your love the finest of all.
Oh fill my heart so, to overflow. For the greatest is Love to show.
Lord give us Hope, in all things to come. For in You, Hope is won.
Help us to never give up on our dreams.
All things are possible through Jesus name... do, do, do, do.

Oh Lord fill me with Your joy... Joy that I can't contain;
Oh Lord, let my cup runneth over, like it pours when it rains.
Like it pours when it rains, Like it pours when it rains.

November 30, 2016

"A man has joy by the answer of his mouth, And a word spoken in due season, how good it is!"
Proverbs 15:23

"You are my hiding place; You shall preserve me from trouble; You shall surround me with songs of deliverance."
Psalm 32:7

"You will show me the path of life; In Your presence is fullness of Joy; At Your right hand are pleasures forevermore."
Psalm 16:11

You Are Wonderful

I just pray Lord that I'm doing what You say.
All the way Lord, that Your light will guide my ways.
Every step Lord, I pray leads me to You.
All my days Lord, till all my days are through.

You are wonderful, the more I read of You.
This I find Lord, each day to be so, so true.
May my faith grow, beyond my wildest dreams.
To see Your face Lord, my soul would surely beam.

May You hear my prayers, each day I raise them up.
May I be worthy of Your love in which I trust.
Keep me steady Lord, to always stay on path.
With Your Words Lord, to guide my every step.

You are wonderful, the more I read of You.
This I find Lord, each day to be so, so true.
May my faith grow, beyond my wildest dreams.
To see Your face Lord, my soul would surely beam.
To see Your face Lord, my soul would surely beam.

January 6, 2017

"Your word is a lamp to me feet And a light to my path."
Psalm 119:105

"And we have seen and testify that the Father has sent the Son as Savior of the world. Whoever confesses that Jesus is the Son of God, God abides in him, and he in God. And we have known and believed the love that God has for us. God is love, and he who abides in love abides in God, and God in him."
1 John 4:14-16

"So then faith comes by hearing, and hearing by the word of God."
Romans 10:17

Frowns Upside Right

You calm the storms in my life.
You turn my frowns upside right.
You are the peace in my night,
And Who keeps my daytimes bright.

You are the One who fights my fights, my Defender in the night.
You break the chains in my life, You give freedom oh so bright.
Oh what a Friend you are, the only One who knows my heart.
Who's known me from the very start, Who's saved my soul, Who'll never part.

You calm the storms in my life.
You turn my frowns upside right.
You are the peace in my night,
And Who keeps my daytimes bright.

Oh what Joy He brings, soothes your soul, frees you from sin.
Your Comforter, your Prince of Peace. No better Friend you'll find than Him.
So seek Him out with all your might, seek and you will surely find.
Knock and the door will be opened. Not one turned away, Christ's arms are open.

He calms the storms in my life.
He turns my frowns upside right.
He is the peace in my night,
And Who keeps my daytimes bright.
He is the peace in my night, And Who keeps my daytimes bright.

January 10, 2017

"Before I formed you in the womb I knew you; Before you were born I sanctified you; I ordained you a prophet to the nations."
Jeremiah 1:5

"Greater love has no one than this, than to lay down one's life for his friends."
John 15:13

"Ask, and it will be given to you; seek, and you will find; knock, and it will be opened to you. For everyone who asks receives, and he who seeks finds, and to him who knocks it will be opened."
Matthew 7:7-8

There Is None Better

There is none better, than the love of Jesus.
He'll fill your heart with treasures and peace within your soul.
Yes, there is none better than the love of Jesus.
This world is not our home, with Jesus we belong... Amen.

Oh to one day see eternity as our Lord has it planned.
Oh what joy will fill our hearts, when at home we are at last Amen.
Oh to see what God has planned and how much He loves us so.
To Behold the beauty of His Love, one day for us all to know Amen.

Yes, there is none better, than the love of Jesus.
He'll fill your heart with treasures and peace within your soul.
Yes, there is none better than the love of Jesus.
This world is not our home, with Jesus we belong... Amen.

Oh the plans He has for us, surely they are good.
I can't wait to see, that mansion in the sky... Amen.
Oh what joy will surely be, in that,
In that sweet, by and by.

Yes, there is none better, than the love of Jesus.
He'll fill your heart with treasures and peace within your soul.
Yes, there is none better than the love of Jesus.
This world is not our home, with Jesus we belong... Amen.
This world is not our home, with Jesus we belong... Amen... Amen... Amen.

February 28, 2017

"See, I have inscribed you on the palm of My hands; Your walls are continually before Me."
Isaiah 49:16

"And we have known and believed the love that God has for us. God is love,
and he who abides in love abides in God, and God in him."
1 John 4:16

"For our citizenship is in heaven, from which we also eagerly wait for the Savior, the Lord Jesus
Christ, who will transform our lowly body that it may be conformed to His glorious body,
according to the working by which He is able even to subdue all things to Himself."
Philippians 3:20-21

"For where your treasure is, there your heart will be also."
Matthew 6:21

Your Grace Abound To Me

In Awe of all I see today, Your Grace abound to me.
Oh where I'd be without Your Love, the dark would surely be.
So thankful now I am to be Your child, I've been set free.
Oh Mercy flows around me now, Your blood ran red for me.

Oh Blessings of that day surround me, I can surely see.
To have Your Love and Hope to hold, well, that changes everything.
Oh a Hope of all made new again, is something to live for.
Without that Hope, days would be grim, so I place my Hope in Him.

In Awe of all I see today, Your Grace abound to me.
Oh where I'd be without Your Love, the dark would surely be.
So thankful now I am to be Your child, I've been set free.
Oh Mercy flows around me now, Your blood ran red for me.

So, I'll work hard in all I do, and Pray I'm pleasing Him.
I'll seek to always do His will and Pray He'll guide me through.
Oh someday I Hope to hear Him say, My child you've done well.
But until that day, He takes me home, well, there's work here still to do.
His Mercy will flow through…. His Mercy will flow through.

May 3, 2017

"And God is able to make all grace abound toward you, that you, always having all
sufficiency in all things, may have an abundance for every good work."
2 Corinthians 9:8

"Therefore, if anyone is in Christ, he is a new creation; old things have
passed away; behold, all things have become new."
2 Corinthians 5:17

"For it pleased the Father that in Him all the fullness should dwell, and by Him
to reconcile all things to Himself, by Him, whether things on earth or things
in heaven, having made peace through the blood of His cross."
Colossians 1:19-20

Jesus My Life Raft

Help me Jesus, I need You so today.
Depending on You Lord, to help me through this day.
Life has its ups and its downs, but with Jesus, Joy still surrounds.
So let the rains just come on down.
I'm grounded in Jesus, my life raft, secure and sound.

So bring on the troubles of this life, bring on the happy let it abide.
All Joy will be for me to see, for in Jesus' hand, I'm held steady.
To battle life's challenges through and through.
God is with me, I'm never alone.

Help me Jesus, I need You so today.
Depending on You Lord, to help me through this day.
Life has its ups and its downs, but with Jesus, Joy still surrounds.
So let the rains just come on down.
I'm grounded in Jesus, my life raft, secure and sound.

I know tomorrow's a brand new day. Yesterday's gone, let the sunshine today.
God has not promised how many my days, so I'll never waste them on worrying away.
I am holding on tight to Jesus, my life raft.
When the waters get high and the wind blows away my sails, God is with me, I'm never alone.

Thank you Jesus, You heard my Prayers today.
I'm standing on Your promises, I'm standing firm today.
I'm standing firm today.

May 13, 2017

"The Lord your God in your midst, The Mighty One, will save; He will rejoice over you with gladness, He will quiet you with His love, He will rejoice over you with singing."
Zephaniah 3:17

"Though I walk in the midst of trouble, You will revive me; You will stretch out Your hand against the wrath of my enemies, And Your right hand will save me."
Psalm 138:7

"This is the day the Lord has made; We will rejoice and be glad in it."
Psalm 118:24

Written Back In Time

A transformation of my mind, when words I read, written back in time.
God inspired, in those days, words for us, to guide our ways.
Blessings from, the Heart of God, Love poured out, to all mankind.
Thankful now, I'll always be, for those words, God gave to me.

There's a softening, of the heart, as God's Word, does fill me well.
The emptiness, that once was there, is filled now, with God's loving care.
There's a hunger now, for His Word, a thirst now quenched, by nothing else.
Than the Father's loving care, and eternity, with Him I'll share.

A transformation of my mind, when words I read, written back in time.
God inspired, in those days, words for us, to guide our ways.
Blessings from, the Heart of God, Love poured out, to all mankind.
Thankful now, I'll always be, for those words, God gave to me.

My eyes fixed now, on things unseen, and faith is the key to everything.
My faith someday, I trade to see, all things God has promised me.
My eyes fixed now, on things unseen, and faith is the key to everything.
My faith someday, I trade to see, all things God has promised me.
All things God has promised me.

June 12, 2017

"All Scripture is given by inspiration of God, and is profitable for doctrine,
for reproof, for correction, for instruction in righteousness."
2 Timothy 3:16

"The Lord has appeared of old to me, saying: 'Yes, I have loved you with an
everlasting love; Therefore with lovingkindness I have drawn you.'"
Jeremiah 31:3

"Now faith is the substance of things hoped for, the evidence of things not seen."
Hebrews 11:1

Here I Am Again

Here I am again on bended knee, one more time to talk to Thee.
Not to ask for anything, only to say thank you.
Thank you Lord, for everything.

As I look around, I see, all these things, You've given me.
Grateful now, my heart does feel, to know Your Love to be so real.
Everywhere I look, I see, Your tender care has followed me.

So, here I am again on bended knee, one more time to talk to Thee.
Not to ask for anything, only to say thank you.
Thank you Lord, for everything.

From a child on bended knee, now adult I surely see.
That Your Love, has followed me and Your Love, has set me free.
Now here I am, with a thankful heart, and here I am, to never part.

July 26, 2017

"For thus says the Lord God: 'Indeed I Myself will search for My sheep and seek them out.'"
Ezekiel 34:11

"Even to your old age, I am He, And even to gray hairs I will carry you! I have
made, and I will bear; Even I will carry, and will deliver you."
Isaiah 46:4

"For the law of the Spirit of life in Christ Jesus has made me free from the law of sin and death."
Romans 8:2

We Cannot Look Away

One evening while working on one of my songs, and trying to get it recorded (I can't remember now, which song I was actually working on, at the time) but, I had the song melody all ready created and memorized, and I was just trying to get it into a finished recording. I had been playing the song, and had been trying to get a finished recording of it for some time, and I was starting to get really tired. I have a bad habit sometimes, of getting distracted, while trying to get a new song recorded. When that red light on the recorder is illuminated, indicating that it is in the recording mode, this always seems to elevate the demands on me – of not messing up, while playing and singing the song. So with that being said, whenever I press that *red record button* on my recorder, and start playing and recording my song, I will usually get to about three-fourths of the way through the song. And then when I get to this point, of where I have most of the song recorded without messing up; that is when I will start thinking to myself – *"I've almost got it… I'm going to get it recorded this time!"* Then that distracts me, and I mess up the recording. I get so frustrated with myself, because if I would just stay focused – just enjoy singing the song, and not think about anything else while trying to record the song, I would get the completed recording much faster.

Well, during that process of trying to get my song recorded, and getting frustrated – I started getting new words on a different subject matter. I started getting new words in relation to staying focused, and not getting distracted, not looking away or thinking about anything else. The words just started coming to me as I was frustrated with myself, and I was saying to myself – *"Come on Sherri, it's like walking on water, you cannot look away. It's like walking on water, you cannot look away."* Then I thought *huh* – that is a very good way of keeping my mind in the right way of thinking while trying to record my song. I thought that the words were a really good lesson for me; so I wrote down those words, and then later turned them into a song. It is one of those songs that just repeats itself, but is also very fun to play.

I feel like the words have a good lesson for life as well. There are so many distractions in this life, that try to pull us away from what God wants us to do; we have to be so very focused, and determined in not getting distracted. It seems to be so easy to get off course these days, and that is exactly what the devil wants us to do. He doesn't want us to complete the things that we feel God has called us to do. We have to fight against his distractions always – *"We cannot look away!"* I have titled this next song: *Like Walking On Water*.

"Raining Clouds with Sun Rays High"

Like Walking On Water

It's like walking on water do, da, do, do, do.
It's like walking on water do, do, do, do.
It's like walking on water do, da, do, do, do.
It's like walking on water, you cannot look away.
No, you cannot look away. No you cannot look away.....

Yes, it's like walking on water do, da, do, do, do.
It's like walking on water do, do, do, do, do.
It's like walking on water do, da, do, do, do.
It's like walking on water, you cannot look away.
No, you cannot look away. No, you cannot look away....

Yes, it's like walking on water do, da, do, do, do.
It's like walking on water do, do, do, do, do.
It's like walking on water do, da, do, do, do.
It's like walking on water, you cannot look away.
No, you cannot look away. No, you cannot look away....

April 28, 2019

"So He said, 'Come.' And when Peter had come down out of the boat, he walked on the water
to go to Jesus. But when he saw that the wind was boisterous, he was afraid; and beginning
to sink he cried out, saying, "Lord, save me!" And immediately Jesus stretched out His
hand and caught him, and said to him, 'O you of little faith, why did you doubt?'"
Matthew 14:29-31

"Let your eyes look straight ahead, And your eyelids look right before you. Ponder the path of your feet,
And let all your ways be established. Do not turn to the right or the left; Remove your foot from evil."
Proverbs 4:25-27

Painted Skies I See

In the Painted Skies I see…
In the Painted Skies I see…
All the grace You've given me.
In the sun I see Your face… Lighting every single day.

In creation I see Your heart… my soul does awe in every part.
In the air I breathe Your love… Each breath I take from You up above.
Oh the mountains high up in the sky. Your hand is strong, Your hand holds mine.
My body's weak, Your strength renews. My soul in need, Your love fills me through.

In the Painted Skies I see…
All the grace You've given me.
In the sun I see Your face… Lighting every single day.

In every step I take each day; Your presence with me here to stay.
I listen close You lead the way. Please help me Lord, to walk Your ways.
When day is done and all is quiet. My prayers I raise to You above.
The moon so bright…. It is Your love. That keeps us safe both day and night.

In the Painted Skies I see…
All the grace You've given me.
In the sun I see Your face… Lighting every single day.

In the Painted Skies I see…
All the grace You've given me.
In the sun I see Your face… Lighting every single day.

In You I rest in Shields of Love… In You I rest in shields of Love.
In shields of Love I rest tonight.

September 25, 2019

"The Spirit of God has made me, And the breath of the Almighty gives me life."
Job 33:4

"But those who wait on the Lord Shall renew their strength; They shall mount up with wings like eagles, They shall run and not be weary, They shall walk and not faint."
Isaiah 40:31

"Of Benjamin he said: 'The beloved of the Lord shall dwell in safety by Him, Who shelters him all the day long; And he shall dwell between His shoulders.'"
Deuteronomy 33:12

"For You, O Lord, will bless the righteous; With favor You will surround him as with a shield."
Psalm 5:12

"God's Eagles Wings Up High, Painted Clearly In the Sky"
"Do You See Them Soaring High? Oh Yes! Soaring High, Soaring High!"

We Must Keep Looking Up

As a child of God, we must keep looking up, awaiting His return. The Bible says that He will return in the same manner to which He left; Jesus ascended into a cloud.

"Now when He had spoken these things, while they watched, He was
taken up, and a cloud received Him out of their sight."
Acts 1:9

Our Lord Jesus Christ could return to us, to take us home to be with Him, at any time. If we are still alive when this event happens – and if we are saved, we will get to see Jesus' return, and we will be *caught up* with Him in the heavens. If we have already passed into Glory, then we will already be with Jesus, if we are saved. So we must make every effort to be ready when Jesus returns, or if He calls us home first. We don't want to miss Heaven, and we can only get there through Jesus! So, when we know deep in our hearts – that we are ready to meet Him in the sky, then we have nothing to fear. When we know that we are ready and right with Him, awaiting His return is exciting, and something we eagerly look forward to.

To meet Jesus face to face – I just cannot even imagine how glorious that will be! Jesus is the Friend of all friends, and the only One that truly knows us. He is Who created us, and Who has been watching over us all of these years. Jesus has been taking care of us; He promises to never forsake us; and He is creating a home for us in *Eternity,* so that we can be with Him forever! He, *Jesus,* is the One that loves us – like no one else can! Oh to see on that Glorious day, for us to see with our own eyes – the scars that He has on His body, from that day so long ago on the cross. Those scars that are on His hands and on His feet, and on His side, *which are the scars that have set us free;* if we will only believe in Him and who He is, and that He died on the cross for our sins, that He rose again on the third day, and that He is very much **Alive** today. If we will believe in Him – we will live with Him forever in *Eternity!* With all that He has done for us, I just cannot imagine what it will be like, when *we* get to meet Jesus – the One that loves us so much; Oh how it will feel to meet Him face to face!

"Therefore you also be ready, for the Son of Man is coming at an hour you do not expect."
Matthew 24:44

"Then they will see the Son of Man coming in a cloud with power and great glory. Now when these things begin to happen, look up and lift up your heads, because your redemption draws near."
Luke 21:27-28

"For the Lord Himself will descend from heaven with a shout, with the voice of an archangel, and with the trumpet of God. And the dead in Christ will rise first. Then we who are alive and remain shall be **caught up** together with them in the clouds to meet the Lord in the air. And thus we shall always be with the Lord. Therefore comfort one another with these words."
1 Thessalonians 4:16-18

Not only should we be watching for Jesus' return, but we should fix our eyes on Heaven, and the things God says He is preparing for us there; the things that, are eternal, versus the things of this earth, which will all perish one day. When we are looking forward to Heaven, I truly believe that it changes how we live here, on this earth. When we know that our time here is temporary, and when we know that we will live there forever; I believe that it changes our goals, and what we strive for. I believe that it will change why we do things, and for what outcome we would like to see out of it. It changes our perspective and our priorities, when we fix our eyes on Heaven our *eternal* home. It causes us also to want to tell others, family and friends, what we have learned; so that all our people, whom we care about, will be in Heaven with us. It will even drive us to care about people, that we don't even know, and cause us to be concerned about their *eternal* future. When we know what the Bible says about these things, of our future in *eternity,* it will wake us up! When we truly understand, that when we die, our souls *will live on somewhere forever,* and that it is totally up to us, by our acceptance or our rejection of Jesus, as to where that *somewhere* will be; when we truly understand this, it should matter to us greatly! Jesus has already done everything for us but we have to receive the gift of Jesus; we have to invite Him into our lives. It is truly amazing to me, how simple God has made salvation for us in these current days, versus Old Testament Times. All we have to do is ask Jesus for forgiveness of our sins; Ask Him to come and live in our hearts; Believe that He is the Son of God, and that He died and rose again three days later; Believe that He is alive today, and then follow Him; Then we shall be saved. And what a wonderfully awesome day yes that will be – What awesome peace shall fill our souls!

"For by grace you have been saved through faith, and that not of yourselves; it is the gift of God,"
Ephesians 2:8

"But when the kindness and the love of God our Savior toward man appeared, not
by works of righteousness which we have done, but according to His mercy He saved
us, through the washing of regeneration and **renewing** of the Holy Spirit, whom He
poured out on us abundantly through Jesus Christ our Savior, that having been justified
by His grace we should become heirs according to the hope of eternal life."
Titus 3:4-7

When we think about the average life span here on earth, if it is God's will, we may live to be in our 80's or maybe longer; well when you compare that to eternity – time without end – there is no comparison! And when you look at the freedom that God has given to us, the freedom to make our own choice, of where we will spend that eternity; well, it seems to me, to be no comparison, and a very easy choice. It seems to be a common sense choice, when we know the truth; when we know that God loved us so much, that He sent His only begotten Son to die for us, so that we might be saved. When we know these truths – it changes everything!

<u>We Have Two Choices, Which God Has Given To Us, The Freedom To Choose:</u>

<u>First Choice: We Choose To Accept Jesus; and God's Plan For Salvation</u> – When we accept Jesus as our Savior, then we will be born again *(a spiritual rebirth)* into God's family through faith in Jesus Christ, and we become *Children of God* with an *Inheritance in Heaven;* with the promise from Jesus, that we will live and be with *Jesus in Heaven for Eternity;* where He promises that everything will be perfect, no tears, no pain, no sorrow; and beauty beyond our imagination. Jesus said that He is preparing a home for us, and that everything will be made new. Jesus even promises to give us new perfect *Glorious Heavenly Bodies.* Bodies that will be like Jesus' resurrected body; His friends knew who He was, He appeared in the room with His friends when the doors were shut; He ate with His friends, and they were able to touch Him. We will recognize family and friends in Heaven, and they will know who we are. We will be reunited with family and friends that have gone on before us. According to the *Scriptures* – Jesus' resurrected body was seen by many people, in those days. *(This first choice is a "Win Win" choice!)*

<u>Second Choice: We Reject Jesus; and God's Plan For Salvation</u> – If we reject Jesus as our Savior, if we do not believe that He is the Son of God, or if we have not made that decision to invite Him into our lives, and to be our Savior; if we die with that decision of rejection of Jesus or lack of acceptance of Him – we will be *eternally* separated from God, and all that, that means – *according to the Scriptures.*

I strongly believe that God is a good God, and that He has given to us, all of this information on future events yet to happen, and has laid them out, and they are recorded in the Bible; because He does love us so very much, and He wants us to know these truths. I pray that each of us will personally do our own research into the *Scriptures* covering this subject; so that we will know for ourselves – the truth. So that we all may know, that our souls will still exist somewhere for *eternity,* after our bodies die; and know that we do have a choice as to where we spend our eternity, according to the Scriptures. And with knowing these truths, that we may have the opportunity to take advantage of these days, make wise choices, and utilize our time well, while we are still here on this earth; during this current and awesome *Grace Period of Time* – which God has given to each of us. From *His Loving Kindness* and *His Grace,* He has given to each of us this awesome period of time, in which we have been given the opportunity to accept Jesus Christ as our personal Lord and Savior.

"For God so loved the world that He gave His only begotten Son, that whoever believes in Him should not perish but have everlasting life."
John 3:16

"For our citizenship is in heaven, from which we also eagerly wait for the Savior, the Lord Jesus Christ, who will transform our lowly body that it may be conformed to His glorious body, according to the working by which He is able even to subdue all things to Himself"
Philippians 3:20-21

"Let not your heart be troubled; you believe in God, believe also in Me. In My Father's house are many mansions; If it were not so, I would have told you. I go to prepare a place for you. And if I go and prepare a place for you, I will come again and receive you to Myself; that where I am, there you may be also."
John 14:1-3

"Jesus answered and said to him, 'Most assuredly, I say to you, unless one is born again, he cannot see the kingdom of God.'"
John 3:3

The words to this next song, came to me one morning while fixing my breakfast, and trying to get ready to go to work. I feel like God was just reminding me, that He is still here beside me and with me, and to not get discouraged; and to keep focused on Him first and foremost! This is another poem that seemed to already have a melody within it, as I wrote the words down. The words came very quickly like all the others, but this one seemed very personal and especially encouraging to me! Later on, when I sat down with my guitar trying to figure out the music part of it – I noticed that this song seemed to be the easiest one yet to figure out, as far as the melody; like I had said earlier, the melody seemed to be already hidden within the words. I pray that whoever is reading this – will be blessed by it! I titled this poem, *Child Don't You Waver*.

Child Don't You Waver

Look to Me child, don't you waver. Keep your eyes on the Son.
Things of this life soon will perish. Will they matter then? No none!

So, keep your eyes upon Me, Jesus. Heaven's home you'll see one day.
Glorious sights will fill your soul, longing you'll feel no more.

So, look to Me child, don't you waver. Keep your eyes, upon the Son.
Things of this life soon will perish. Will they matter then? No none!

So, keep your eyes upon Me child. Live your life for Me alone.
Look no more to things of worry. Close your eyes you're almost home.

Glorious days you'll one day enter, filled with sights you've never known.
And your life filled with much pleasure, days on earth no more your home.

So, look to Me child, don't you waver. Keep your eyes, upon the Son.
Things of this life soon will perish. Will they matter then? No none!

So, look to Me child, don't you waver. Keep your eyes, upon the Son.
Things of this life soon will perish. Will they matter then? No none!
No none!

September 26, 2019

"Looking unto Jesus, the author and finisher of our faith, who for the joy that was set before Him endured the cross, despising the shame, and has sat down at the right hand of the throne of God."
Hebrews 12:2

"Simon Peter said to Him, 'Lord, where are You going?' Jesus answered him, 'Where I am going you cannot follow Me now, but you shall follow Me afterward.'"
John 13:36

Oh What Joy

One of these days… Lord we'll meet You face to face.
Oh what joy… our souls will embrace.
In a land of Glory... No more tears on our face.
Yes, one of these days Lord we'll meet You… Yes, we'll meet You face to face.

Yes, one of these days Lord we'll meet You, and Glory will fill our eyes.
And we'll walk on streets of gold… with You along our side.
And sadness & sorrow will be there no… no… no…
Only joyous reunions of loved ones gone on before.

One of these days… Lord we'll meet You face to face.
Oh what joy… our souls will embrace.
In a land of Glory... No more tears on our face.
Yes, one of these days Lord we'll meet You… Yes, we'll meet You face to face.

Oh is Jesus your Savior? Is He your closest Friend? Do you trust Him with your life,
And ask your sins forgiven? Oh is Jesus your Savior? Do you wait on His return?
Is your heart filled with joy? Does His Comfort soothe your soul?
Oh is Jesus your Savior? Do you wait on His return?

One of these days… Lord we'll meet You face to face.
Oh what joy… our souls will embrace.
In a land of Glory... No more tears on our face.
Yes, one of these days Lord we'll meet You… Yes, we'll meet You face to face.

Oh yes, Jesus is my Savior… and He's my closest Friend. And I trust Him with my life.
And have asked my sins forgiven. Oh yes Jesus is my Savior… and I wait on His return.
And my heart's filled with Joy and His Comfort soothes my soul.
Oh yes, Jesus is my Savior and I anxiously await … His return.

One of these days… Lord we'll meet You face to face.
Oh what joy… our souls will embrace.

In a land of Glory... No more tears on our face.
Yes, one of these days Lord we'll meet You... Yes, we'll meet You face to face.
Yes, we'll meet You face to face.

June 28, 2020

"The twelve gates were twelve pearls: each individual gate was of one pearl.
And the street of the city was pure gold, like transparent glass."
Revelation 21:21

"And God will wipe away every tear from their eyes; there shall be no more death, nor sorrow, nor crying.
There shall be no more pain, for the former things have passed away.'" Then He who sat on the throne
said, 'Behold, I make all things new.' And He said to me, 'Write, for these words are true and faithful.'"
Revelations 21:4-5

"If we confess our sins, He is faithful and just to forgive us our
sins and to cleanse us from all unrighteousness."
1 John 1:9

Through Jesus We Are Made Strong

Everything doesn't have to be perfect in our lives; we just need *Jesus,* and *His Peace,* and *His Joy, and His Comfort,* in the center of our lives, for our lives to be good. If we get that priority right, *Jesus in the center,* all other areas of our lives will be in its perfect harmony. You see, Jesus is who helps us to stay strong: He gives us just the right Scriptures, sends the Holy Spirit to dwell in us – to keep us standing strong through – whatever life brings us. Through **Scripture** we gain **wisdom** on how to handle life; and through **Jesus,** we are made **strong;** what a **Victorious** way to live and find true **Peace!** Jesus is always the answer! He created us – He is our maker, and He knows all things! I go to Him with all my prayers, and He is so faithful to supply all my needs! I am so thankful that we have the **Hope of Jesus!** I wouldn't want to live any other way. I just can't imagine not having the **Hope of Jesus.** He truly is the **HOPE** of the world! Thank you Jesus for being our **SAVIOR** and our **HOPE** in all things today, and in to **ETERNITY!**

"Lantana Flower Plant: Possibly God's Example in Nature of How We Should Spread the Gospel."
In researching this plant, I have found that once it has been introduced into certain regions, it can spread quickly. In addition this plant is also, in some cultures, a symbol of Happiness and Joy!

We Need You Lord

Oh we need You Lord… Every hour, every day;
Yes, we need You Lord… From the beginning of the day;
Till at night we lay our heads.
Yes we need You Lord.

Oh when things are going good;
And we think the road is smooth.
Lord never let us forget;
Oooh we need You Lord.

Oh we need You Lord… Every hour, every day;
Yes, we need You Lord… From the beginning of the day;
Till at night we lay our heads.
Yes we need You Lord.

Lord never let us be unarmed;
Never let us, let our guard down.
Lord remind us, that You are near.
Oooh, we need You Lord.

Oh we need You Lord… Every hour, every day;
Yes, we need You Lord… From the beginning of the day;
Till at night we lay our heads.
Yes we need You Lord.

Oh that devil passes to and fro; To destroy our lives as we know.
Lord, let us know that You are here.
Oooh, we need You Lord.

Oh we need You Lord… Every hour, every day;
Yes, we need You Lord… From the beginning of the day;
Till at night we lay our heads.
Yes we need You Lord.
Oh, we need You Lord. Yes, we need You Lord.

January 25, 2021

"Therefore take up the whole armor of God, that you may be able to
withstand in the evil day, and having done all, to stand."
Ephesians 6:13

But I Know

The world's a scary place; and our days are ever changing.
But I know the Lord, is always with me;
And I... will not be shaken!
For He, is right beside me... Psalm 16:8 reminds me.

So, I will be at peace; and my soul will be in comfort.
Because my eyes are on His Glory; and the Heaven He's preparing.
Yes my eyes are on His Glory; and the Heaven He's preparing.

The world's a scary place; and our days are ever changing.
But I know the Lord, is always with me;
And I... will not be shaken!
For He, is right beside me... Psalm 16:8 reminds me.

So, if a day upsets your comfort; or a moment brings a heartache,
Remember all His promises, and His love is always with you.
Yes, remember all His promises, and He is always with you.

The world's a scary place; and our days are ever changing.
But I know the Lord, is always with me;
And I... will not be shaken!
For He, is right beside me... Psalm 16:8 reminds me.
Psalm 16:8 reminds me.

May 11, 2021

"I have set the Lord always before me; Because He is at my right hand I shall not be moved."
Psalm 16:8

"Fear not, for I am with you; Be not dismayed, for I am your God. I will strengthen
you, Yes, I will help you, I will uphold you with My righteous right hand."
Isaiah 41:10

Jesus truly is our strength! When we have the helper *(the Holy Spirit)* in us, to help guide us: He encourages us, strengthens us, helps us in times of trouble, comforts us, and gives us courage; we are made strong through Him! He, the Holy Spirit, also helps us to remember Scriptures, when we encounter difficulties in our lives; and these Scriptures will help us, and guide us in the right direction in which we should go. When we have read or heard God's word, then when we are up against an obstacle in life, or if we are trying to help someone else with something that they are going through, the Holy Spirit will remind us of these things that we have read; and these Scriptures will help us to navigate through our problems. Just like writing this book, I don't have all of these Scriptures memorized that I am sharing, I wish that I did; but I do know that the Bible says these things, I just can't remember them exactly. But the Holy Spirit is reminding me of them, these things I have heard or read previously, as I am writing this book.

"But the Helper, the Holy Spirit, whom the Father will send in My name, He will teach
you all things, and bring to your remembrance all things that I said to you."
John 14:26

So then, when these Scriptures come to my mind, as I am writing, I will find that certain verse that I was thinking of in my Bible, so that I have the verse quoted correctly to share in this book. Like I said, I am very unqualified for the task that I feel God has given me to do. But I do believe that God is helping me along, in my efforts of trying to accomplish what I feel, He is directing me to do. And I absolutely believe that He will do the same for each of us, if we will just ask Him to. When I have finished this book, one of the things I would like to start doing, is to try to memorize some of my favorite Bible verses that I have included in these writings; so that I have them correctly hidden in my heart.

When We Truly Seek To See

This next song, I think is probably my Mother's favorite song, out of all the songs that I had written at that current time; this is the one that she felt was anointed. This song came to me quickly just like all the others; but, what was different with this one is that, when I sat down to try to figure the melody part out on my guitar, the melody and chord progression came exceptionally fast. As well as, on that same day that I laid down the chords to this song, and was practicing it – I felt like I could probably get it recorded. So with that being said, I turned on my little hand held recorder, pressed the *record button,* and if I am remembering correctly – the first try to record it, I got it. Now remember earlier, I had shared that I had to work and work for hours, trying to get a song recorded without any mistakes; usually it would be several days of trying before I would get a good recording. Notice I did not say a perfect recording. Because all of the songs which I have recorded have something in them that I wish I could change; but we are not perfect human beings, and I have done my best with them. I think that is all we can do, is to do the very best that we can, and then leave the rest up to God. I titled this next song – *All Around Me.*

He truly is *all around us!* When we truly seek to see, the evidence **is** all around us! May we all be *blessed* every time we look around to see *God's Creation.* "And you will seek Me and find Me, when you search for Me with all your heart." (Jeremiah 29:13)

"The entrance of Your words gives light; It gives understanding to the simple."
Psalm 119:130

"The Evidence of God's Existence Is Truly All Around Us – In His Creation"

All Around Me

Jesus in me… all around me…
Jesus Savior, Redeemer and Friend.
Jesus today and tomorrow…
Yesterday into Eternity!

Oh who would want to… Go a day without Him…
Oh the blessings that surrounds Him…
In my days I want Him always…
In my moments and my tomorrows.

Jesus in me… all around me…
Jesus Savior, Redeemer and Friend.
Jesus today and tomorrow…
Yesterday into Eternity!

Oh the Blessings that surrounds us…
In our joys and our heartaches…
Every moment that God gives us…
It is Jesus that does ground us.

Jesus in me… all around me…
Jesus Savior, Redeemer and Friend.
Jesus today and tomorrow…
Yesterday into Eternity!

May our eyes be open always…
May our souls be full of love…
To not miss what does come our way…
Blessings from our Lord above.

Jesus in me... all around me...
Jesus Savior, Redeemer and Friend.
Jesus today and tomorrow...
Yesterday into Eternity!
Yesterday into Eternity!

May 19, 2021

"If you love Me, keep my commandments. And I will pray the Father, and He
will give you **another** Helper, and He may abide with you forever."
John14:15-16

One Sunday morning while watching my favorite Bible teaching program, I started getting the words to this next song. So while still in my pajamas that morning – I went back to my music room, and started writing the words down. The original writing was a little messy, because I did not have my glasses on yet – *I am so very thankful for all the people that have invented things, and that do the jobs that help to make our lives easier, and healthier* – like glasses so that we can see, for one example! I titled this song: *Creator Of My Soul.*

Creator Of My Soul

For my eyes will be on Him; The Creator of my soul.
Yes my eyes will be on Him; The Creator of my soul.
As I walk this earth… I know.

In all He's done for me; my soul is ever grateful.
In all He's done for me; I'll praise His name forever.
Yes, in all He's done for me… How could I not… Praise Him.

Yes, my eyes will be on Him; The Creator of my soul.
Yes my eyes will be on Him; The Creator of my soul.
As I walk this earth… I know.

I'm forever grateful; To the Creator of me…
Yes, I'm forever grateful to our Father in Heaven…
Yes, I'm forever grateful; to the Creator of All things…

Yes, my eyes will be on Him; The Creator of my soul.
Yes my eyes will be on Him; The Creator of my soul.
As I walk this earth… I know.
Yes, my eyes will be on Him… Hmmm
Yes, my eyes will be on Him… Hmmm
Yes my eyes will be on Him… Hmmm
As I walk this earth… I know…

May 30, 2021

"For You formed my inward parts; You covered me in my mother's womb. I will praise You, for I am fearfully and wonderfully made; Marvelous are Your works, And that my soul knows very well."

Psalms 139:13:14

This next song is probably one of my favorite songs to play. I believe it is, because it opens my eyes every time I sing it and play it, to all of the beautiful things that God has created for us to enjoy. I feel *Peace* within, when I see the evidence of God's presence in His creation! I pray that, this song will bring that same *Peace* as it is being read now, as well.

Jesus Is Everywhere

Jesus is everywhere... He's in the rising of the sun; and the stars we see at night.
Yes, Jesus is everywhere... He's in the voice of the birds; and the beauty of their songs.
Yes, Jesus is everywhere... He's in the fragrance of the flowers; and their beauty held so bright.

Yes, Jesus is everywhere...
He's in the beauty of the setting sun; in the clouds hung fluffy and white.
Yes, Jesus is everywhere...
In our days... and our nights.

Jesus is everywhere... He's in the rising of the sun; and the stars we see at night.
Yes, Jesus is everywhere... He's in the voice of the birds; and the beauty of their songs.
Yes, Jesus is everywhere... He's in the fragrance of the flowers; and their beauty held so bright.

Take time to look around... keep our eyes open wide.
Don't let the busyness of the day...
Steal what God.... has for us...

Jesus is everywhere... He's in the rising of the sun; and the stars we see at night.
Yes, Jesus is everywhere... He's in the voice of the birds; and the beauty of their songs.
Yes, Jesus is everywhere... He's in the fragrance of the flowers; and their beauty held so bright.

Yes, Jesus is everywhere...
In every single breath we take; and every breathtaking waterfall,
In the love of a twinkle...
In a puppy's eye...

Yes, Jesus is everywhere.... Yes, Jesus is everywhere....

June 25, 2021

"And He is before all things, and in Him all things consist."
Colossians 1:17

"Jesus Truly Is In – The Beauty of the Setting Sun"

There is so much on God's green earth to see – Jesus' presence truly is everywhere! It is quite amazing to me – of how much seems to catch my eyes these days! It is so wonderful in these current times, with the technology we now have a camera with us built into our phones, at all times. The things that we can capture in nature and share with others, is endless when we are looking to see – to see all that God has created! For us to notice His creation, whether it is in the sky or it is on the ground; it is truly breathtaking and awesome to take in! Let us always be looking for that little something that God has put out there for us to enjoy; I promise that if we look every day, we will see something along our path, that God has created just for our enjoyment! For when we are enjoying and admiring God's creation, we are also enjoying and admiring the Creator of it – *Our God and Father in Heaven!*

"Sitting So Cute With Lunch in Hand – God Supplies All Our Needs – We Understand"

Make Me Aware

Lord Jesus… help me find You in this day.
Lord make me aware of Your presence along the way.
Lord heal any hurts that I may have;
And leave only praise in my heart to stay.

Oh in this world, there'll be heartaches;
But Jesus came to save. So just let them brush away;
Like a feather floats along… On a breeze…
That carries it away.

Lord Jesus… help me find You in this day.
Lord make me aware of Your presence along the way.
Lord heal any hurts that I may have;
And leave only praise in my heart to stay.

Jesus promises… that He is here.
Right beside us, in all our days… to this promise we all hold tight.
With all our heart and all our might;
To Jesus' Words… I hold tight.

Lord Jesus… help me find You in this day.
Lord make me aware of Your presence along the way.
Lord heal any hurts that I may have;
And leave only praise in my heart to stay.

So, I will look for Jesus today...
And I'm sure I'll find Him along my way.
His creation is everywhere... beauty we see; Oh what Hope it... plants in me.
Of what Heaven's creation... of beauty... must surely be!
Lord Jesus... Help me find... You... In this day.

June 27, 2021

"Seek the Lord and His strength; Seek His face evermore!"
1 Chronicles 16:11

"Have I not commanded you? **Be strong** and of good courage; do not be afraid,
nor be dismayed, for the Lord your God is with you wherever you go."
Joshua 1:9

Lord Keep Me

Lord, keep me in tune with Your love for me to know.
For there's nothing in this world, that ever compares to You.
Lord, help me to see what is true and real.
For nothing else is worth the loss of You.

For in this world are many things to pull our attention to.
Distractions they are everywhere that try to pull us from You; that try to pull us from You.
So pull us back to You Lord, for this is where we thrive.
To have Your love along our side, that's when we feel alive; That's when we feel alive.

Lord, keep me in tune with Your love for me to know.
For there's nothing in this world that ever compares to You.
Lord, help me to see what is true and real.
For nothing else is worth the loss of You.

For this world You made for us, and in it we do live.
But we are not from this world, our souls created for You; Our souls created for You.
Our home is not in this world, we're merely passing through.
So let us not lose our souls, by distractions in our view; by distractions in our view…

Heaven bound we truly are… our souls in You alone.
For one day You will call us home.
And Home we'll surely be.
Cause we're merely passing through….

April 27, 2022

"Behold what manner of love the father has bestowed on us, that we should be called children of God! Therefore the world does not know us, because it did not know Him."
1 John 3:1

"That we should no longer be children, tossed to and fro and carried about with every wind of doctrine, by the trickery of men, in the cunning craftiness of deceitful plotting."
Ephesians 4:14

"If then you were raised with Christ, seek those things which are above, where Christ is, sitting at the right hand of God. Set your mind on things above, not on things on the earth."
Colossians 3:1-2

Write It Down

I believe that God is always very active and interested in our lives. We just have to trust Him and trust what He is doing in our lives. He does not reveal the whole big picture to us; it is definitely a moment by moment journey. The best way for us to follow Jesus is through the direction of His word.

"Your word is a lamp to my feet and a light to my path."
Psalm 119:105

"Being confident of this very thing, that He who has begun a good work
in you will complete it until the day of Jesus Christ;"
Philippians 1:6

So with that being said, when that soft inner Voice starts speaking to us – a direction of something for us to do – it is good for us to follow it, if it follows scripture, and if it is a good thing to do. Our days are made up of all these moments in time; and each thing that we do, leads us to the next thing to do. So if we are following in the direction in which we think the Lord is leading us, if we don't continue to follow that soft inner Voice – we just might miss what is just around the corner; the future event that God has planned especially for us. Something wonderful! We can't get to the other side of the project without starting the project. And I truly believe that whatever God starts in us He will bring us through; and all these things that we do will glorify Him! I would have never thought that I would be writing a book, and sharing my story now; but, when that first poem started entering my mind I had to write it down, and then the next one came, and I wrote it down. Then before I knew it I had an overflowing amount of poems that had been written in a very short amount of time. Where did this all come from, and why? All I know is that I wasn't doing anything that seemed to be all that important until I started looking to God for the answers – then everything started to shift, to have more of a spiritual importance. All of a sudden things seemed to be leaning in a different direction, a direction that felt like God was taking the lead, instead of me leading my life. It seemed as though God was giving me something to do, that I could share, that would maybe make a difference in the lives of other people, or maybe something I could share that would possibly inspire someone to want to know what God has for them.

But what is most interesting to me now, is that through all of this journey of writing down all these poems, and now trying to write a book so that I can share them; and in the process of searching His word to find that perfect scripture that lines up with each of the poems to be entered into the book – well, I feel that God is ministering to me all over again through this process. In the same way that He has ministered to me through the poems in the beginning, but now even to a deeper level; because as I am searching His word, the poems that I feel He has given to me, are now taking me deep into His word. Somewhat like the heart of the watermelon, the super sweet part of the watermelon; I feel like God is taking me into the heart of His word. It is quite *amazing* how God works through us, and it has been a very *inspirational journey for me!*

When we feel that God may be talking to us, we should let Him lead the way whole heartedly, in whatever direction we feel He is calling us. We just never know where He is leading, and what may be just around the corner. We have to just keep on taking that next step!

I started writing this book on the day of September 16, 2018. Many additional moments have happened since that day. At that time, I thought God just wanted me to write about the first CD of songs that I had completed in 2017. I had no idea that there would be three more CDs to write about. I am guessing God had a different plan! I am now finally bringing this book to its completion, and it is now five years later. I would have never imagined! And I am so thankful that I kept taking that next step, and very thankful for this journey in which God has me in the middle of now!

This next song speaks of that very journey of – *taking the next step.* I was just playing my guitar one evening, and working on one of my other songs, when the following words started coming to me – *"If you feel a song a coming… write it down; If you don't, you'll surely miss what's coming round."* So … LOL, I wrote those words down! Then, that same evening, I just started playing around with some different chords on my guitar, and singing those words. It seemed to be coming together, so I decided to record it, and make it a song for my fourth CD. Those words spoke volumes to me, because of my own journey. This song just repeats itself, but I didn't feel like it needed any other words. I pray that it will inspire whoever is reading it.

The *"song"* – for someone else to write down – could be anything that God may be laying on someone's heart to do. This song for me is about what God has given me to do; but, it could be anything that God is laying on someone else's heart for them to do. Is God whispering a *"Song"* to your heart, for you to write down?

Write It Down

If you feel a song a coming... write it down. If you feel a song a coming... Write it down.
If you don't... you'll surely miss... what's coming round.
If you feel a song a coming, write it down. If you feel a song a coming, write it down.
If you don't, you'll surely miss... what's coming round.

If you feel a song a coming, write it down. If you feel a song a coming, write it down.
If you don't you'll surely miss... What's coming round.
If you don't you'll surely miss... What's coming round.
So, If you feel a song a coming, write it down. If you feel a song a coming, write it down.
If you don't ... You'll surely miss ... what's coming round.

So, if you feel a song a coming ... write it down. If you feel a song a coming... write it down.
If you don't... you'll surely miss... what's coming round.

So if you feel a song a coming... Write it down. If you feel a song a coming... Write it down.
If you don't ... You'll surely miss... What's coming round.

June 25, 2022

"Listen to counsel and receive instructions, that you may be wise in your latter days. There are many plans in a man's heart, Nevertheless the Lord's counsel – that will stand."
Proverbs 19:20-21

So By Faith I'll Walk

This journey that I feel God has taken me on, for sure these last eight years, has definitely been a *Walk of Faith;* a communicating back and forth of prayer to our Heavenly Father up above. I know deep in my heart that He hears our prayers, and I want to encourage whoever is reading this book, to never give up on God! Even though sometimes it may feel as though He is not listening, keep praying, and keep praying, and keep trusting, and *keep believing!* Pour out your heart to God, from the bottom of your heart with all that you have in you – with whatever is on your heart that you may need prayer for! I promise God is listening, and just when we may think that all hope is gone, Jesus steps in; He is listening, and *He hears our prayers!*

But we always have to remember – it's all in God's timing; He is the only One that knows all things – we sure don't! God blesses us, and answers the prayers that line up with His will, which Glorifies the Father in Heaven; which is also the best for each of us overall, and in to *Eternity!* God is our Creator, and He always knows what is best for us, and we have to trust Him with – *His all knowing!*

> "Most assuredly, I say to you, he who believes in Me, the works that I do he will do also; and greater works than these he will do, because I go to My Father. And whatever you ask in My name, that I will do, that the Father may be glorified in the Son. If you ask anything in My name I will do it."
> John 14:12-14

I want – what Jesus wants for me; because, I for sure do not know what is best for me! I believe that whatever we have planned for our own lives, just doesn't even compare, to what God's predestined plans are for us – so, *I trust Him with my life!* We are not God, only God is God; and He is a wonderfully good God, who wants to bless us, when we love Him and are trusting and believing in Him!

> "For I know the thoughts that I think toward you, says the Lord, thoughts of peace and not of evil, to give you a future and a hope."
> Jeremiah 29:11

There are troubles in this world – no doubt! But these troubles – are just the things that bring us to our knees, and cause our souls to go running to Jesus! We are all in dire need of a Savior! Without the troubles in this life, we would never know – how desperately we need a Redeemer!

"These things I have spoken to you, that in Me you may have peace. In the world you
will have tribulation; but be of good cheer, I have overcome the world."
John 16:33

God was so gracious to give us a wonderful mind, and the ability to make our own choices. He wants us to trust in Him! I believe that He could, in a blink of an eye, change all of our hearts to love Him; but how empty would that be – to just create us that way. He wants us to need Him – to love Him, and trust in Him because we choose to love Him; because He first loved us! God draws us to Himself with His lovingkindness and His Grace, and His Mercy for us, through the gift of Jesus His Son!

"The Lord has appeared of old to me, saying; 'Yes, I have loved you with an
everlasting love; Therefore with lovingkindness I have drawn you.'"
Jeremiah 31:3

"I call heaven and earth as witnesses today against you, that I have set before you life and
death, blessing and cursing; therefore choose life, that both you and your descendants may
live; that you may love the Lord your God, that you may obey His voice, and that you may
cling to Him, for He is your life and the length of your days; and that you may dwell in the
land which the Lord swore to your fathers, to Abraham, Isaac, and Jacob to give them."
Deuteronomy 30:19-20

Jesus promises us a perfect new heaven, and a new earth, when He makes all things new; this is where we fix our hopes, and look forward to all things being perfect and good! This is the place where we will finally have peace for all eternity; we will be satisfied there, when we are finally and safely home! That glorious home that God is creating for us – there, will be our peace! So, while here on earth – we hold tight to Jesus' promises, *His Word*, His precious promises to us, and to the instructions that He gives us. We place our trust in Jesus, and then – one day, one glorious day – we will all enjoy awesome peace evermore with family and friends, and with Jesus there, and a love that will satisfy all our needs! I know He hears all our prayers! The more we draw near to Him, the closer He draws near to us – so, keep praying, keep praying – ***keep praying!*** Jesus loves us with an ***everlasting love*** – like none we have ever known!

Christianity is a personal relationship with our Lord and Savior Jesus Christ. Jesus is also the closest Friend we will ever have! We have been given the awesome privilege to be able to talk to Jesus anywhere, and at anytime. Jesus Loves Us – and desperately wants to hear from us, and He wants us to love Him; He also wants to be a part of our lives, and to be our Savior! His desire is to spend Eternity with us – Please take advantage of this awesome privilege and **talk to Jesus today!**

As I was re-reading and double checking my writings in the previous paragraph; I just got this very calm and peaceful feeling of Jesus' presence with me – I just stopped and enjoyed that awesome feeling! Jesus is so kind and generous to us, what an **Awesome God We Serve!**

"And He came and preached peace to you who were afar off and to those who were near. For through Him we both have access by one Spirit to the Father. Now, therefore, you are no longer strangers and foreigners, but fellow citizens with the saints and members of the household of God,"
Ephesians 2:17-19

"Nevertheless we, according to His promise, look for new heavens and a new earth in which righteousness dwells."
2 Peter 3:13

"For we walk by faith, not by sight."
2 Corinthians 5:7

"Now faith is the substance of things hoped for, the evidence of things not seen."
Hebrews 11:1

"By faith we understand that the worlds were framed by the word of God, so that the things which are seen were not made of things which are visible."
Hebrews 11:3

"If you abide in Me, and My words abide in you, you will ask what you desire, and it shall be done for you. By this My Father is glorified, that you bear much fruit; so you will be My disciples."
John 15:7-8

"But also for this very reason, giving all diligence, add to your faith virtue, to virtue knowledge, to knowledge self-control, to self-control perseverance, to perseverance godliness, to godliness brotherly kindness, and to brotherly kindness love."
2 Peter 1: 5-7

I Know He Hears

I raise my hands ... Way up high... And I pray... To my Father ... Up in the Sky.
In all His power ... He does reign... He hears our prayers... He knows our pain.
And I know... He hears all prayers... we're praying here.

So, I'll never give up, even though I don't see. God's timing is His, not for me to know.
So by faith I'll walk... and by faith I'll see... One day God talking to me.

So... I raise my hands ... Way up high... And I pray... To my Father ... Up in the Sky.
In all His power ... He does reign... He hears our prayers... He knows our pain.
And I know... He hears all prayers... we're praying here.

So while here on earth, I'll just keep on, keeping on, as I feel He's leading on.
I'll keep moving along... One day I'll see, in Eternity.

So... I raise my hands ... Way up high... And I pray... To my Father ... Up in the Sky.
In all His power ... He does reign... He hears our prayers... He knows our pain.
And I know... He hears all prayers... we're praying here.

But for now the journey ... is to enjoy, Life and all He's given ... With Joy in our stride.
Tell others about Jesus ... whenever we can ... Keep looking up ...
No never look down.

So, I raise my hands ... Way up high... And I pray... To my Father ... Up in the Sky.

July 9, 2022

"I love the Lord, because He has heard my voice and my supplications. Because He
has inclined His ear to me, Therefore I will call upon Him as long as I live."
Psalm 116:1-2

"Look upon me and be merciful to me, As Your custom is toward those who love Your name. Direct my steps by Your word, And let no iniquity have dominion over me."
Psalm 119:132-133

Life Has Purpose

"Without God – Life Just Repeats Itself, Like an Old Wagon Wheel Going Round and Round"
"But, With God – Life Has Purpose, and With Him, We Can Make a Difference"

"Wisdom is good with an inheritance, And profitable to those who see the sun. For wisdom is a defense as money is a defense, But the excellence of knowledge is that wisdom gives life to those who have it."
Ecclesiastes 7:11-12

"For the Lord gives wisdom; From His mouth come knowledge and understanding;"
Proverbs 2:6

"He who gets wisdom loves his own soul; He who keeps understanding will find good."
Proverbs 19:8

In Conclusion

Whatever our God given predestined purpose is – I believe that it will have a trail or a path behind it – leading up to it, equipping and preparing us for what God created us to do; I believe that it is probably in a constant state of setting up, you might say. From what I can see, with my own life story – of my hobbies, and things I thoroughly enjoy doing, as well as, with what I have learned in the jobs that I have had; I believe all have equipped me to do what I feel God is calling me to do now. I am so grateful for this trail behind me, and very thankful for what I am getting to do in these current days! I am sure that there are other Christians that have had, or are having now, similar experiences; and many other Christians that will get to experience this process, of finding God's will for their life, and noticing what experiences have equipped them for it, along the way. I am certain that every experience we have in our lives is either, teaching us something that will help us, and/or equipping us to help others; as well as, enabling us to tap into the hidden gifts that God has given us long ago – before the earth was even created. Scripture tells us, that God had planned and thought for each of us specific purposes, in this special time designated just for us to do – at this precise time in the earth's history. Have you ever thought of that? Why are we here, right now – in this current time exactly? God's purpose – is the conclusion that I have come to.

"And He has made from one blood every nation of men to dwell on all the face of the earth, and has determined their preappointed times and the boundaries of their dwellings, so that they should seek the Lord, in the hope that they might grope for Him and find Him, though He is not far from each one of us;"
Acts 17:26-27

We all have a purpose – something that God has preplanned for each of us to do for His Kingdom. It could be something as simple as going over, and giving a person who is mourning the loss of a loved one – a hug from above at just the right time; that it might be of some comfort, and maybe make a difference in someone's future wellbeing; which may help them to have peace and comfort in coping with their loss; and then knowing deep inside, that you had the feeling, that the Holy Spirit had directed you to do just that – give that hug! All I know – is the best path that has been for me – is to read my Bible, and use it as my guide; pray, and then ***Trust Jesus*** in all circumstances. Listen to that ***Soft Voice***, and follow it as best that I can; and ask for God's Blessing and Protection over everything and every person in my life; then wait and watch for God to work in my life.

When we do something, that we feel God is telling us to do for someone – then, when we get to feel the fulfillment of the reaction from that person, which confirms God's directions to us – it is truly an awesome and satisfying feeling; it will leave us wanting to experience that again and again! When we get to experience one of these spiritual moments, it will make us feel all tingly all over, as if the Holy Spirit is dancing all around us; it is a wonderful feeling! I truly love the things that I believe God has given me to do; these are the moments in time when I feel the most alive! A purpose driven life keeps us moving forward, enjoying life with an opened eye, trying not to miss what God has destined for us to do – is truly amazing!

I believe that God has planted a spiritual seed within all of us, and that it is up to us to take care of it, nurture it, and encourage it to grow. It is up to us to make sure that we are spiritually fed, so that we may grow into the person God created us to be. Jesus is there to help us, absolutely, but we have to allow ourselves to hear His word, so that we may grow spiritually; and arrive at a place in our lives, where we will desire God's word as our survival, and a necessity for our everyday lives! We have to thirst for the relationship with Jesus, He will not force that on us; we have to open the door to our hearts, and invite Him in.

I believe Jesus is constantly seeking after us; but we have to accept Him as our Savior! Then we will have in us, the Holy Spirit to guide us along, direct us on the right path, and help us when we need it. With the *Holy Spirit* in us as our guide, and *God's Word (Scriptures)* with us and in our hearts; we will then have all that we need, to navigate through this life – and in to *Eternity!*

I pray for God to continue to give us the courage and the strength, as we try to follow Him and His will for us, to the best that we are able. As well as, that He may increase our *Faith* and our *Wisdom,* as we are journeying through this precious life, which God has given to each of us. And may we always do our very best to *Glorify God* in all that we do!

"From His Glory, For His Glory, None Other"

Sincerely,
Sherri L. Land

"With God – Our Hope Is Always Bright"

May It Go

This book I pray
With God's Blessings

Will be to all
Which God had predestined

To far and wide
May It Go

To bless their souls
And raise God High

May it accomplish All
That God had intended

And Encourage God's people
To Chase...
The Dreams within Them!

August 22, 2023

"In Stillness Resting"

Prayer of Salvation

If you are not a Christian, and would like to become one, I ask that you would please pray this prayer with me.

Dear Jesus,

I know that I am a sinner, and I need You in my life. I want to change the course of my life; I want to turn from my sins, and follow You. I believe that You are the Lord Jesus Christ the Son of God, and that You came to this earth because You loved me so much. I believe that You died on the cross for my sins, and that three days later God raised You to life, so that I may have a new hope, and eternal life through You; and that if I accept You as my Savior that I will be with You in heaven for eternity. Lord Jesus, please come live in my heart forever. Please forgive me of my sins, and be my Savior; I invite You into my life. Please help me to be transformed into the person that You created me to be, so that I may Glorify You for all eternity. Thank you Jesus for being my Savior, I love you Lord, in Your Precious Name, Amen.

If you have prayed this prayer – I pray that you will tell someone what God has done for you, and share with someone that you are now a Christian – because you have asked Jesus to come and live in your heart, and to be your Savior.

For anyone who may have prayed this prayer, and is now a new Christian – You have just made, the most important decision, you will ever make in your entire life; an awesome decision to be joyfully excited about! And I am extremely happy for you! May God's Blessings surround you, in your new Christian walk! May the Peace of God be with you always, and may His presence fill your soul completely!

"For all have sinned and fall short of the glory of God,"
Romans 3:23

"For the wages of sin is death, but the gift of God is eternal life in Christ Jesus our Lord."
Romans 6:23

"The thief does not come except to steal, and to kill, and to destroy. I have come that they may have life, and that they may have it more abundantly."
John 10:10

"Therefore, having been justified by faith, we have peace with God through our Lord Jesus Christ,"
Romans 5:1

"For God so loved the world that He gave His only begotten Son, that whoever believes in Him should not perish but have everlasting life."
John 3:16

"Behold, I stand at the door and knock. If anyone hears My voice and opens the door, I will come in to him and dine with him, and he with Me."
Revelation 3:20

"That if you confess with your mouth the Lord Jesus and **believe** in your heart that God has raised Him from the dead, you will be saved."
Romans 10:9

"For 'whoever calls on the name of the Lord shall be saved.'"
Romans 10:13

May God Bless All Who Have Read These Writings

And May He Fill Their Hearts with the Peace and Comfort of the
Presence of our Lord Jesus Christ;
As They Proceed On Through Their Own Life Journey Ahead...

"Now may the Lord of peace Himself give you peace always in every way. The Lord be with you all."
2 Thessalonians 3:16

I have one last moment in my story that I would like to share. On August 15, 2023, I was having a little trouble sleeping. I was probably about a quarter to half way through of writing this book. My mind just didn't want to shut down. I think a lot of it was, just being super excited about writing the book. Whenever I have trouble sleeping, I try to think on what heaven will be like, and what it is going to look like; this usually relaxes me, and I go to sleep. But this particular night, I started getting words instead. I tried to keep lying there, and just go to sleep but the words were so comforting to me that I had to get up, and write them down. So as not to wake my husband by turning on the light, I went to the kitchen, and tried to find a pen and scrap paper by the night light we leave on over the stove. Finally, I found a blank area on the back of a postcard advertisement, and with pen in hand at 1:31am by the light of the stove, I wrote down the words that were entering my mind. These are the words that I wrote in that early morning hour. I felt like it was the Holy Spirit comforting me, so I titled it: "A Bedtime Prayer from the Holy Spirit."

A Bedtime Prayer from the Holy Spirit

Sleep little children close your eyes
The Holy Spirit in you does reside
Stay your mind on Heavenly places
And Peace be with you till you rise
And Peace be with you till you rise.
Amen

"God's Wonderful Sun Setting In Sun Rays"

"'Behold, God is my salvation, I will trust and not be afraid; For YAH, the Lord, is my strength and song; He also has become my salvation.'"
Isaiah 12:2

"When you pass through the **waters,** I will be with you; And through the rivers, they shall not overflow you. When you walk through the fire, you shall not be burned, Nor shall the flame scorch you. For I am the Lord your God, The Holy One of Israel, your Savior;"
Isaiah 43:2-3

About The Author

Sherri L. Land was born and raised in Kansas. Sherri has been married to her husband for forty-five years, and has been blessed with two wonderful children, and four awesome grandchildren. She has worked as an Administrative Assistant for an accumulation of thirty-five years, and has recently retired. Sherri is a child of God, who has trusted God for as far back as she can remember, to a little girl. Until one day God got her full attention, and He changed the center of her life to be totally focused on what, she felt God was calling her to do, going forward. Since that crossroad in her life, through much prayer, she has written well over one hundred poems. Sherri has also self recorded forty-two songs, within four CDs, which are all recorded in the Library of Congress. Through the years she has self produced many copies of those CDs, which she has shared with family and friends. Sherri also enjoys drawing and taking photos of God's creation. She is writing now, her very first book titled: *How His Light Shines Through Us "This Is My Story"* all the while praying for God's Blessings over it, and through it.

Milton Keynes UK
Ingram Content Group UK Ltd.
UKHW050644151024
449462UK00018B/22